RITISH NANCHAHAL

UNDERGROUND ENTREPRUNERS' SECRETS

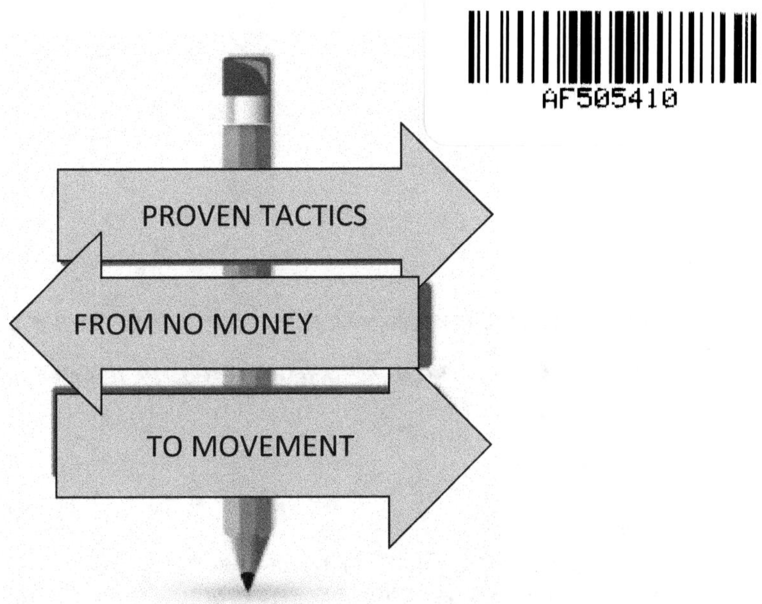

Devoted to all
Non Venture Online Startups with No Safety Nets

Ritish Nanchahal

This is a work of nonfiction. No names have been changed, no characters invented, no events fabricated.

For more information, visit nanchahalconsultations.in
or search "Ritish Nanchahal" on Google

Devoted to all non venture startups with no safety nets

PRELINES

VISION IS A FORCE THAT ALL FUNNELHACKERS ARE DRIVEN FROM

No matter they sell coaching or product at their DOTcom (.com)

Our business is our child and strategy is the upbringing

Each step, each action is going to take intense change to his future

Thinking smarter and overdilivering is our art-form

When passion creates impacts, that's how funnel-hackers are born from

WE ARE FUNNELHACKERS AND THIS IS OUR GAME......

Devoted to all non venture startups with no safety nets

<u>DEDICATION</u>

To my dad, who helped inspire me to become an entrepreneur. To my mom, who always knew my true worth.

My sister, who made me polish on my skills by saving internet and for supporting me through all of my crazy ideas, made me to chase my dreams.

Devoted to all non venture startups with no safety nets

CONTENTS

Devoted to all non venture startups with no safety nets

Devoted to all non venture startups with no safety nets

UNIT:-1
CLEANZING THOUGHTS AND ATTITUDE

Devoted to all non venture startups with no safety nets

<u>ACKNOWLEDGEMENTS</u>

There are so many people I want to thank for being willing to share their ideas with me. Ideas that ultimately became the strategies behind everything inside of this book. I also want to thank my team— all the people who helped me to implement these ideas, find out which ones work, and share them with the world. While there are hundreds of marketers I have learned from, there are many people who gave me very specific ideas that built the framework for my company, and also for this book. I've tried to give credit to the original sources when possible, but some of these people may be left out. So I want to mention a few of the brilliant marketers who have inspired me in no particular order. Russell Brunson, Sam Ovens, Tony Robbins, Dean Graziozi, Steven Larsen and everyone else who has taken the risk to be an online entrepreneur and provide value online!

Lastly, I want to thank my Family. These people have given me the ability to try all of these crazy ideas, and share in the successes and the losses.

Devoted to all non venture startups with no safety nets

WHAT THE SUCCESSFUL STARTUPS AND ONLINE ENTREPRENEURS FEDRATION DOES NOT WANT YOU TO KNOW? AND IS THIS BOOK A FRAUD?

Yes, there IS an 'ONLINE STARTUP ENTREPRENEURS FEDERATION. Many of them hang out together, scheme together, and work together. And yes, there ARE a few things they'd rather you didn't think about, while they perform their wizardly shows. This book is going to reveal those underground secrets and filled with tons of energy and motivation that pushes you to chase the ultimate abundance Don't misunderstand. Few of these wizards are actually evil. Most bring valid 'magic tricks' to the show. Many do guide business people to treasure. But often there is a discernible pattern behind everything they say, teach, promise,

Devoted to all non venture startups with no safety nets

9

and promote: a deliberately-engineered and exacerbated lack of solid ground. This book doesn't just focus on magic tricks, but the some strategies you have to have in place to start and scale a company with online media as well as the motivation which will keep you driven to the journey of making your dreams reality.

Being 17 today and founder of 3 successful startups made me able to share the knowledge and stuff that I implemented in my business and created a movement in the online market. I am not a famous Social butterfly, My Instagram is in state of paralysis. I do not have twitter or snap chat account, I refused to download that on my devices, but what made me to get those results consistently that was in my dreams some years before and consistency of learning and implementing.

While teaching you about the "shiny" secrets of the Internet, I will show you how to build these tactics and strategies into your business on solid ground— tactics and strategies founded in true direct-response marketing.

I'm for challenging norms and breaking rules. But I also like solid ground, not ever- shifting sand. I like being confident and in control of things—

particularly my money and the making of it—not in constant high-anxiety and at the mercy of wizards.

I taught myself direct marketing as a science as well as an art. I like reliability . I'm far more interested in a car that starts and runs well and predictably every time you turn the key than one that looks sexy and is popular with some in-crowd, but might stall at 80 MPH or not start at all. I like evergreen, not frequently obsolete. In my roles as a strategic consultant and a direct-response copywriter, I am all about creating advertising, marketing, and sales assets of lasting value for my clients—not moneymaking devices written in disappearing ink.

Discipline is good. General Norm Schwarzkopf (of Operation Desert Storm fame) once said:

"Shined shoes save lives."

   RITISH | **NANCHAHAL**

This book offers solid ground in the very ethereal world of online marketing and lead generation. It properly treats Internet media as media— not as a business. It utilizes the power of startups' motivation and examples to prove the strategies correct. It builds on long-proven marketing funnel and sales architecture. It takes a very disciplined approach. You will not become a funnel master after reading this book, I am not sharing everything, but you will became the grand master of the funnels discussed inside, I promise. It is, in one way only, a fraudulent book. The title is deceptive. It really is not about "Underground secrets of entrepreneurs" nor is it a playbook for "growing your company online." It is that, but such a narrowed and limiting characterization is deceptive.

In truth, this is a solid book about reliable movement and marketing 'secrets' that can be applied to online business activities. In truth, this is a proven playbook for growing your company with effective lead generation and sales/conversion methods, which can be used online and offline.

Don't go into this book in lust for a new, cool, quick, easy "fix" or nifty "toy" or clever gimmick that might make you money today but require you to find another and another and another, at frantic pace. Go into this book in search of deep understanding and profound clarity about the structure and science of effective marketing and understanding soul of the business. Art behind to be applied in the online media universe.

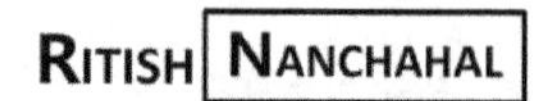

WHAT THIS BOOK IS ABOUT (AND WHAT IT'S NOT ABOUT)

Hey, my name is Ritish Nanchahal ... Before we get started, I want to introduce myself and let you know what this book is about (and more importantly, what it's not about). This book is NOT about getting more leads through your website—yet in the lead funnel section I will share with you the killer lead capture tools that make me 1200 per day per site organically. This book is NOT about increasing your conversions—yet these secrets will break your beliefs, but this will wash away the misconceptions in people's mind regarding funnels and business.

If you are currently struggling with getting started with your ideas, or converting that ideas into a successful business online, you may think you've got a problem. In my experience, after working with many businesses, I've found that's rarely the case.

Getting panic at startup is a common issue with most businesses and this creates the difference between million dollar businesses and those who never ever seem to came into existence, even the ideas was same for both.

Peter Theil: founder of Pay-pal and many million dollar companies said -"A business messed at startup, cannot be fixed." His friends call it THE THEIL'S LAW.

Moving Forward, If you already have a business: Low leads and weak conversion numbers are just symptoms of a much greater problem, a problem that's a little harder to see (that's the bad news), but a lot easier to fix (that's the good news). 3 months before (that time I was on fundamental stage of learning funnels, before I was working on e courses and webinars) I get a chance to contact Neha Agarwal, From Mathematical inclined, you can watch her videos on YouTube, a great Mathematics teacher and I shared with her my dreams and goals. She researched on my links and suggested me to work on execution. I asked her How?, She replied me, As MacDonald and KFC do. I took that suggestion seriously and Then I keenly researches on both of the startups, in my way I get chance to learn about Starbucks, Oyo Hotels and Subway's story as well.

Take Subway, for example. Subway used to be just another fast food restaurant like McDonald's, Burger King, and all the rest. Then somewhere along the line, the company found this guy named Jared. He was a big guy who weighed over four hundred pounds.

However, he started eating nothing but Subway twice a day, and over the course of a couple of years, he lost a ton of weight. Subway shared Jared's story with the world. They put him in commercials, on billboards, everywhere. Just by this tiny little approach, Subway transformed its business from an average fast food restaurant to a weight-loss plan. This new tactic completely set the company apart from the competition. One of the reasons that Subway does so well is because it focuses marketing tactics around a customer's experience. People trying to lose weight can relate to Jared. They understand his backstory, and they want to be like him. If this guy could lose all that weight just by eating Subway twice a day, then they can too. This same guy has been bringing in business for Subway for over fifteen years!

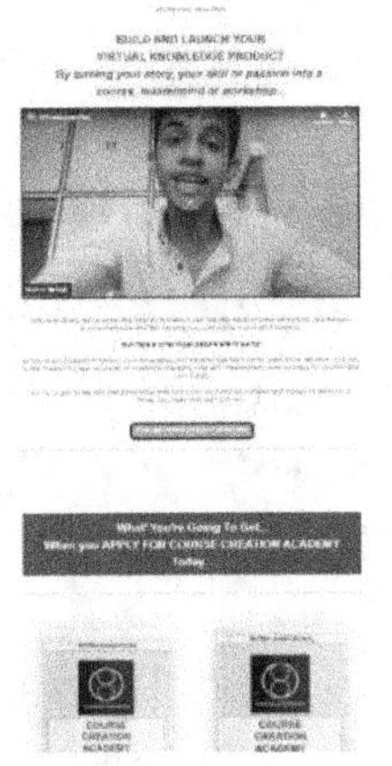 

Then I applied the same approach. I was working on my coursecreationacademy.co.in where I am teaching in 7 days, the way to convert your silly idea or skill to a proper paid course that you can sell to others for years. I was not getting much sales of it, So I changed the message from CREATING A E-COURSE to HOW TO UNLEASH THE HIDDEN KNOWLEDGE CURRENCY, YOUR PASSION AND SKILL AND TURN IT TO SOMETHING THAT CAN IMPACT LIVES AND MAKE YOU PASSIVE INCOME.

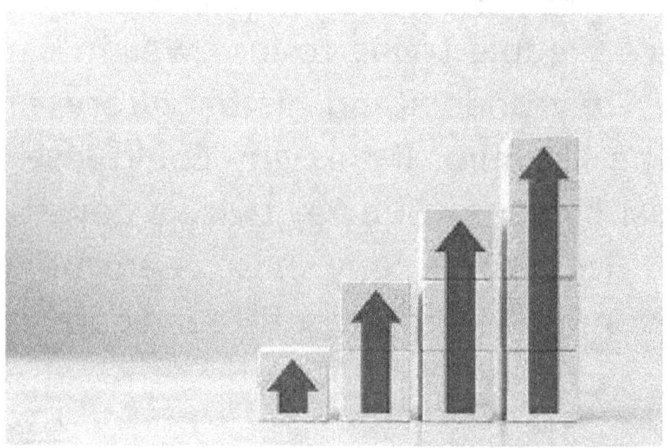

Boom! Overnight my sales doubled. Then I changed my Course selling website to a Funnel, Again Damn, it boosted up the sales and today that particular funnel is making 1200rs on an average per day by selling 3 course bundles of 400 Rs daily.

I smiled because that's why most people call me. They usually assume that I'm going to help them tweak a headline or change their ad targeting, and solve their problems. But I knew that, like most companies problem wasn't a traffic or conversion problem. It rarely is. More often than not, it's a FUNNEL problem.

After listening to coaches and consultants' all of their numbers, their pains and frustrations, and their ups and downs, I sat back in my chair and told them they were in luck. "You don't have a traffic or conversion problem," I said. "What are you talking about? Our traffic is down 90%, and we can't break even converting our customers!" They said.

"The problem is with the way to sell, problem is your lame sales funnel," I replied calmly. One of them was ready to invest on a new office but was confused about to invest in sales funnel. I told him; One of my mentors, Dan Kennedy, says, "Ultimately, the business that can spend the most to acquire a customer wins."

So, what changes did I make to their businesses? How did I take a sales funnel that was losing money and transform it into a tool that allowed them while gaining more traffic, more customers, and more sales? THAT is what this book is about.

In first section you will go through some of the foundational lessons, experiences that I learnt from my failures and after wastage of a lot money, effort and energy and that Ido not want you to repeat the same mistakes. Also we will uncover the profound soul of a successful business. I am a rule breaker, so together we will try to break misconceptions and that brick walls that forces us to calm down and live average. Then in second part we will jump to the strategies and tactics. Here we will discuss art and science behind successful businesses and funnels. In last portion we will deeply dive in funnology and I will show you the case study of my own lead capture funnel.

When you implement each of these secrets, you will transform your business and your website from a flat, two-dimensional, company (looking like a brochure) into a three-dimensional sales and marketing machine that allows you to outspend your competitors, acquire an almost unlimited number of new customers, make (and keep) more money, and most importantly, serve more people. That is what this book is about.

Devoted to all non venture startups with no safety nets

RITISH NANCHAHAL

INTRODUCTION

My business creating addiction began in class 6th when I tried to sell my old toys and books to children and successfully sold my old books set for rs 1500, (that price was higher than the market price of old). I was very happy to do that sale and it was like blind hits the mark. I started to think every thing and process in profitable way. I started to notice that how businesses work, how sales is made. I watch my father daily that he makes sales of thousands and even lacs, when he was in car selling company on phone calls. Being frank, I never learnt that process from my father. In home, the discipline of a teacher and student lacks, also I was not able to invest money on high ticket coaching and masterminds.

It was a vague approach, but I bought a pen-drive and started to download video lessons of my classes from youtube and started burning that data on DVDs by using local computer cafes. I sold its first copy to my school friend, who never ever focused on studies, but was in panic state at time when exams are near. I sold that DVD set for rs 200. This is how I sold my first E Product.

Devoted to all non venture startups with no safety nets

I was a too introverted guy, that's why, when other children of my age were playing cricket or football, I was in my home. I take a pen and a copy and do mimicry of my teachers. This induced interest of teaching in me. I used to play teacher -teacher with my little sister and it polished my skills. I started to teach tuition to younger students and that damn feel of having an authority of the class, was a great confidence booster. In my class 9, I was teaching tuition to students of class 8 and was making money.

I became stable, teaching 4-5 students in a batch with 2 batches a day was something I was feeling fulfilled with.

One day cleaning store room, probably in class 10, yes it was class 10th, I found some books of my dad, he bought many years ago, but never read it, ha!ha!, but it was interesting for me to go and read something from it. I found a book of T. Harv Eker "SECRETS OF THE MILLIONARE MIND." I did not know what happened but I started to read it. As I was reading page by page, it was , it was really opening new gates of wisdom for me. I fall in love with its manuscript and the way he was telling the mindset if millionaire. I learnt concepts like mental files and folders, mental blueprint and many amazing things. I have also made a podcast episode on that Mental files right now.

I did not know how, Maybe my fascination grew because it was so charismatic. Whatever the reason, as soon I read its one chapter, I try to save that memory in form of visual content, so I started a youtube channel "#vr learning world." Its now not available. But literally I started to grew my channel organically, I reached lum sum, probably 86-87 subscribers in 2 months, but it was an amazing experience for me, I put my mother's phone camera in hand, with other hand, I teach and doodle the concept I learnt on a copy with pen. This is how I met Mr. Vimal. He was amazed with the way I was describing and that's how in 1 week from getting on WhatsAap, we were in front of each other, discussing our ideas and goals.

During this talk, he told stories about how he started his first business. He explained how he came up with decision of learning french and graduating with English honors after doing non medical. While most people wouldn't consider that a big win, but he was clear with his thoughts, and that's what I liked him about the most.

I didn't realize it at the time, but ,Mr Vimal was teaching me (and everyone else who was present) that the ideology and being responsible for decisions and results is very important to create your worth.

Well, as you can guess, my 15-year-old eyes opened wide, and my heart started racing. I remember getting so excited that I couldn't sleep that night— or the rest of the week. All I could think about was creating a business so I could start making money.

But a successful business model can never be perfect at startup. I Was working on my processes and strategies, but I was more caring the people's comments and feedback. What people feel then they visit my site? What Motivates them to buy? What creates an impact. Business and services are the weapons and ways, but people pay to you, to listen you. If today somebody else will come and handle my clients, maybe he knows better tactics then me, clients would be uncomfortable with him.

Mrs Rekha Shahani, she is a lady creating a massive impact. She works with the British Council for their Core Skills Programme. She is associated with IOFC as the Core team member of 'ETST - Education Today, Society Tomorrow'. She also serves as an elected member of the Asia Pacific Coordination Group (APCG) of the IOFC that works in developing nations towards the goals of facilitating education, leadership, building trust and sustainability along with reconciliation. She is the Diplomatic Secretary of the Early Childhood Association & APER. She helped me to find best colour scheme and tell me which headlines will suit in my course creation academy sales page and covid mindset toolbox, that I was using to get leads for my course creation academy programme. I do not met her directly. She used to give teaching seminars and training sessions, and In one of her workshop series, my mother was present, that's how I got her known from my mother, then I contacted her and told about my dreams and aims and how I want to impact world with my services, she was happy and she blessed me whatever I was doing.

I still remember when my cousin Varinder came to me and told me about a entrepreneur named Sam Ovens and forced me to watch all his videos available on YouTube. He found that spark in me, he was trying to fuel that little tiny spark to create a big business firestorm. I was not so serious that time, frankly, I thought He dropped out from college, but he was having financial safety and no worries, but If I will walk on his footprints, it may be fatal. But he was mature to understand that I can invest that energy, whatever I was burning on random tasks and watching TV to learn and create something new. I was living in life of dreams, but he was living in practical reality that time. I still remember going with him on a drive and he surprised me with a laptop and provided me recordings of courses and mastermind events, so that I can start learning business and create one for me. I was not expecting this from him, my family also requested him that please take it back, since at that time, we were not in a financial state that we can pay back the money, but as he forced us to take it and pay back whenever you get it, I took the case seriously. I started to invest regular time to learn business, entrepreneurship and started doing sales calls, My heart was racing as I started to learn from Sam ovens. I started taking notes and doing worksheets as Sam told to me in his Course. And that is where this journey began for me, that's how I first stepped into professional consulting business. I can never pay him back the feel, the effort he putted in me at the right time, thanks man!

Also being an INTJ, Whatever I said was just a Thank you and gave him a hug, I did not know, how to express my feelings and tell him what I think, Being INTJ Himself, he can understand better.

Devoted to all non venture startups with no safety nets

I started to collect and read mails, magazines, PDF, books and started to learn from masterclasses and events, in my journey, I found People like Russell Brunson, Dean Graziozi, Tony Robbins etc. From Rusell Brunson, I learnt the concept of sales funnels, and here I got my niche. Today I have all of his paid courses and books, from where I created my stuff and services. The way, how he was doing it, and it was fascinating to me. Whatever he was selling, the process was the same.

Russell's team members; They are asking people to contact their company for a free report. After you contacted them, they would send you a sales letter, disguised as a free report, selling a low-ticket information product. When I purchased the product, they sent me their "subscription"—along with another sales letter email selling me a high-ticket product. This was my first exposure to sales funnels. I didn't know it at the time, but this process I was seeing over and over again offline would become the exact SAME system that grown hundreds of companies online.

Looking back, I think it's funny that while most kids my age were collecting baseball cards, I was studying courses and mail and learning marketing funnels. That's the place from where I started and today helping coaches to multiply their leads and conversions using sales funnels without spending tons of time, money and effort on programmers and strategists.

The storm is near and now is the right time for you to create an impact too.

OUR MOTIVATION IS EXACT OPPOSITE

I became part of a subterranean Tribe of entrepreneurs you probably never heard of before, the companies that started from scratch, the one man armies that started from a phone and a laptop, and changing the world with their services consistently.

We don't rely on cash from venture capitalists to get started and we don't even have goals to go public either. In fact our motivation is the exact opposite, you see we have products and services and things that we know change people's lives because we're fighting against the big companies and brands, with those people that have literally unlimited budgets. So we have to do things differently. We have to take actions smarter. We don't have financial safety and backups because every test we take, got invested with our own money from our own pocket. So We have to be profitable from day number one

How we do that? How is that even possible? Something that you will never learn in your college books, something that those people will tell you that what you are going to do is impossible.

Doing self evolution each day, iterating the processes, Understanding by heart the art and science behind a successful startup.

We call it funnel hacking and the people who do that are known as funnelhackers. It's not really something that I can explain to you. Something I have to show you stories and glimpse of entrepreneurs just like you who have a dream and a vision, who want to change the world in their way. We use this funnel hacking process and they'll make their dreams become reality.

Oh yes! we are funnel hackers and this is our game........

Entrepreneur by birth, 'X' by choice.

You are an entrepreneur by birth, but what you are by choice? …

Here you will:-

- Find out what the difference is between a regular entrepreneur and a Funnel Hacker.
- Hear an emotional story about how entrepreneurs can change people's lives when they are super passionate about their art..
- And find out what mantra Ritish and The funnel Doc are going to push for the next 12 months, and why it matters.

What's up everybody, This chapter I am writing to you from depth of my heart, I'm taking a much needed mastermind retreat and break after a busy duration. But I wanted to do a couple of special talks , while I'm out, out of the usual schedule. I think I'm technically still in The schedule actually, Yep, I cannot live free, but from reference of usual schedule I am feeling little relaxed, free and away from the busyness.

Obviously I'm not going to write all my feeling here, but there were some key ones that I really did want to share with you guys. ....

In fact, some of my PowerPoint presentations from the first day of this funnel business, which I'm really proud of, that I wanted to get in the mindset of all of our Funnel Hackers. I'm going to share with you guys right now. So the next text will be part of my presentations. First off, I wanted to talk for a little bit about what a Funnel Hacker is. What makes you a Funnel Hacker? In fact, T-shirts are available with the tagline "Entrepreneur by choice, but Funnel Hacker by birth."

So what is a Funnel Hacker, excused me, flip that around, "Entrepreneur by birth, Funnel Hacker by choice." That makes way more sense. So you're born as an entrepreneur but you chose to be a Funnel Hacker. So what does that actually mean? What did you choose to be part of? Why do you listen to me, why do you listen to my webinars, why do you use Funnels, what is the difference between a typical, traditional entrepreneur and a Funnel Hacker?

So I'm going to have Russell Brunson grab that part of the text and share it here for you guys to read to and hopefully it helps you guys to understand a little bit more about the community and about who you are, why you are here, why you're different, why a Funnel Hacker is different from a traditional entrepreneur and why that matters Her is literally a genius person that popularized the concept of sales funnels and taught me in my learning hours.

Russell Brunson once was actually at a wrestling tournament with his kids and he was watching his kids saw somebody who had a shirt on that said, "Athlete by birth, wrestler by choice." He remembered seeing that and he was like, 'Oh my gosh." That called to me and I started thinking about it in this context. When I listened to this incident, it was again like "oh my gosh." I said, all

Devoted to all non venture startups with no safety nets

the people that use funnels are entrepreneurs right, you guys were all born that way.

And that's how this tagline "Entrepreneurs by birth, funnel hacker by choice" came to existence. But it is not just a cool tagline, it have a deep meaning behind.

I'm curious, for each of you, when was it in your life that you were sitting there and you realized that you were a little bit different? Do you remember the first time you're sitting there and you're like, 'I think I'm different. I think differently than all the people sitting around me in the classroom." Do you guys remember that, that moment?

I remember sitting in class in my school, I'd be sitting there and the teacher would be talking and I was like, "I don't understand what they're saying." And I'd look outside and see the office, where our director was having the charge of supremacy and I was like, 'I just want to go there and create and do similar stuff. To be being a founder was not only the motivation, money was also a second goal, but the thing that most enthusiast me was CREATING AN IMPACT. The founder of School has not just made money, she has not just devoted her life to sit on a chair of supremacy, do daily tasks, take stress

Devoted to all non venture startups with no safety nets

for growth and rule on the staff and else, but the self fulfilling motivation, pushes her to move forward and set some visions that SHE IS IMPACTING THOUSANDS OF LIVES DAILY. As a teacher, she is making students to stand on there feet and chase their dreams. As a Authority, she has given ways to teachers to earn finances. As a mother, she has made her children live the life with full of abundance and respect and a lot more. I'd be fidgeting in my seat in classroom and it was hard to pay attention, and I struggled. I struggled through school, as a lot of entrepreneurs do. But something clicked at last month of session always, that I complete my classes with good grades, was strange.

And I remember all through junior to high, all through higher classes and even through coaching, thinking I was dumb. If people ever asked me, "What are you studying?" "Oh I just study Business. They call me fool, since I was in non med stream, but I was reading stuff regarding commerce. I don't care about any of them, I was only focused, to do something in my life that will create infinite possibilities for the future generations.' And the reason why I always had that response is because I always thought I was dumb, I just assumed that I was, because I couldn't understand what the teachers were saying, I couldn't memorize the things they were telling me and then regurgitate them and I was usually absent on tests, and all those things were really hard for me. But since I was polite, out of the box thinker, and respect every teacher, I was having a good image in my school.

And it wasn't until towards the end of my class 11th when I started learning about this world, about entrepreneurship, about what was possible, and it was the most exciting thing in the world for me, I'm sure it's the same way for a lot of you guys, especially some of you guys who are newer, just kind of starting to learn about business, and starting to feel that excitement and that joy.

I remember sitting there listening to some people that I met who were starting businesses and I hear them talk about it, and every single minute it was like Diwali, it was so exciting. And I remember that as I'd start learning things, even up to senior secondary boards, I didn't think I was a reader. I didn't like reading, but I think it was because most of the books I read weren't interesting to me. But I still remember the very first time I read a book, it was a business book and I learned a principle, and I was like, "That's interesting." I took that principle and I applied it to my business, and I saw my business grow. I was like, "Oh my gosh, that is the most exciting thing in the world. I learned something, I applied it, and I made more money."

And I was like, "I want to learn something else." So I read another book, and I'm like, 'There's three cool things. Let me try that." I tried this, this, and this. I tried it and my business grew and I was like, 'This is the most exciting thing in the world. This is like a treasure hunt every single day." And I got into reading and studying and learning and going to events because I was looking for every one of these little gold nuggets I could get and apply to what I was doing, to help what I was doing grow. It become a habit of mine, reading books, attending webinars, downloading courses. When guys of my age were used to download cracked version of GTA, PUBG Etc, I was too passionate about to build my knowledge currency and downloading recordings , workbooks, presentations of mastermind events and watching them till midnight. And that's when I realized that I wasn't dumb, I was just not interested in the same things that other people were. I was interested by growth, by business, it was the most exciting thing in the world for me. I remember a chat, My friend congratulated me for the success I was getting by helping coaches online to grabbing more leads and selling high ticket using funnels, and she said me that you are really lucky. It hit me, I replied that When you were hanging out in birthday parties, I was reading books, when you were listening to memes, I was listening to my clients' issues, when you was enjoying the world, I was creating the world, If that means Lucky; Yes, You can call me "LUCKY"

I think for a lot of you guys, if you're here reading this book you're probably the same way, am I right. You guys were born as entrepreneurs but you're here today because of a choice you made. A lot of people hear the entrepreneurial call, the call to contribution, as Alex Charfen calls it. We hear the call to contribution, we know that we want to do something, we want to create something, we want to give, we want to serve. But a lot of people don't listen to that, they ignore it, and they forget about it. But the fact that you guys are here reading this book means you heard the call, and then you made a choice and said, "I'm going to do something about it. I'm going to start a business. I'm going to take this idea, I'm going to take this thing, I'm going to create it. I'm going to do something different."

And so while you're an entrepreneur by birth, you are a Funnel Hacker by choice. That's why you guys are here with me today. And to me the only people that can change this world by their services and coaching are FUNNELHACKERS. I'm so excited to be here with you guys.

So the question then is, what in the world is a Funnel Hacker? We can find Funnel Hackers from all around the world, these are some of the kids in Kenya that we build schools with. They wear Funnel Hacker t-shirts, last time I came out, I got Funnel Hackers everywhere. So what is a Funnel Hacker? Outside of this world, people don't know what that means. So I want to kind of define what it means to me, and hopefully what it means to you as well.

We recently made a new manifesto and I'm going to kind of go through this, but this is the Funnel Hacker manifesto. I believe it's on the back of your guys' programs as well. So I'm going to talk about, I'm going to kind of break this down, piece by piece. So the first thing here is the Funnel Hacker is a new breed of entrepreneur, they're smarter, leaner, faster, and free.

What's interesting about this community. Think about an event you come to, everyone is coming there with their own businesses. They are money driven commonly, they will present their services, if the frontier is not interested, they will leave him and try to approach another one. I don't put people into business, this is not a business opportunity. What this is, is you guys all have businesses, we've got businesses from every range of the spectrum. People that have, there's dentists, there's chiropractors, there's people that are Lasik surgeons, there's people that sell courses, there's people that do coaching and people who do live events. There's every kind of business you can dream of, physical products, people doing franchises. It is insane how many businesses come into this world. Under the Roof of Funnel hackers, you will find them all together and happy with each other's friendship. They do not share services and money, they share motivation, story, they want to grow, but most specially, they want to grow together.

The Funnel Doc (my company) is not something that creates businesses, that's not what we do. What I do is we are a tool and a training platform to help your business go faster. I do not want that you come to me, pay me and get my products and services, I want that you will get some spare time, out of your day and spend it with your family, I do not want you to get rid of door to door selling, But I want that let the online funnel do it and you invest that energy to create another product, or service for your customers that will help them to solve some problem and impact the world. That's what I do. So as a Funnel Hacker, when you come into this world, you have to understand that our goal, our mission is to help you take whatever it is you've already got, that's your business, your job, and our job is to help you to amplify it, to make it go faster. That's the mission I have, that's what we stress about all the time. How do we do that, how do I make it so the entrepreneurs can move faster and faster and faster?

So as I was going through this, Funnel Hackers are the new breed of entrepreneurs, what does that actually mean? And I started thinking about it. The Funnel Hackers are the people in this room, not people that are like, "Oh yeah, I've got a business." Do you understand that you don't just have a business, but you are insanely passionate about your business? The thing that makes you different than a typical entrepreneur, a typical business owner is that you are obsessed with your thing. Every one of you guys have your own thing, you have your own business, whatever it is that you do, and you're obsessed with it. You want to be the best in the world at it.

The dentist or the mechanic, or the small business owner who is not obsessed is not here. They are at home doing the thing. You guys are here because you're obsessed with it. You want to do more. You're obsessed with the thing. You look at your thing as your art. Some of you went to school for your art. Some of you guys have learned it on your own, but it's your art. Do you guys feel like what you do, your business, is your art? Yes. I feel the same way, our business is our art, our creation. Its like a kid we are feeding daily and caring like a genuine infant. This is what we're doing, what we're giving such a huge percentage of our life to, and if we don't believe in it that much, then we're in trouble.

So the first thing is that Funnel Hackers are obsessed with their thing. And the second thing, and this is what really differentiates you guys, is that you are also, not only obsessed with your thing, but you're more obsessed with the marketing of your thing. You understand that no matter how amazing your art is, if nobody sees it, then what good is it. It hasn't helped anybody, hasn't changed anybody's life. It's because of that that you come here to learn how to market your art. I can't make you guys better at what you do, but I can make you better at getting the word out about what you do.

That's what's different. That's what we do here. That's the first step.

Number two, a Funnel Hacker believes that their business is a calling. Do you guys feel like your business is a calling? A Funnel Hacker believes that their products, their services, and the messages they share have the ability to change the lives of the people that they have been called to serve. I want to tell you guys a personal story about a business owner, an entrepreneur, somebody who believed this.

The day, I am going to host my first webinar. Before it, let me tell you an incident, one day In my class 6, one day I forget to take out the lunchbox from my bag and was unluckily having some left off veggies remaining, the next day, when lunch break started, I opened the lunch box and saw, woooo! is that the yesterday's lunchbox, suddenly my teacher announced that the students that will not take their whole meal will be punished, you all have to learn to finish the food. I was scared, I thought what do I do now? I was confused, Though I was too introverted, I was ashamed of telling the teacher my case, The feeling of being ashamed that I forget to change my tiffin and fear of going against teacher's command pushed me, and I really ate those rancid veggies that day. I do not know, how this nerd, who was too introvert, is going to host a webinar with audience and will try them to sell stuff.

So after I started to host the webinar, it was insanely cluttered. As I started I found there are only 4 people who are going to attend the session with me. Since I have learnt stuff from people who have 20-30 thousands webinar attendees, I was a little depressed, but my mother supported me emotionally by teaching that you cannot expect roof, until you have not crossed the staircase, today you have 4, next time maybe 10, next to next time, more, this is how they will increase. So I become confident and I started to host that session. Before the session I was too excited, I made registration site working, I made a whole workbook prepared, I created banner etc, etc, etc, but inside the session I found people were nodding off, they were not paying any attention to the stuff I was teaching. I was blasting with tactics, and they were taking it as a chapter of civics.

So this response created huge amount of anger, and I shouted to the height and dapped the table with full force by saying, "Do you know how much, time, effort, energy and money costed me to learn all the stuff what I am telling to you for free, I have learnt it from some of the top entrepreneurs of globe and I have attended this this this this event, I have read this this this this this book and I have created this this this this service from it that is going to impact world, are you mentally present to engulf all that!"

Suddenly all of them got fully alert, they came to knew that what is the value the stuff I was teaching really hold. They understood that how I really learned and earned it, and that's how I grabbed there attention. Then I learnt from that experience that you should never burst the techy stuff, you have to match your frequency with your audience frequency, then when it started resonating, then you can leverage the level of energy, it will increase efficiency of that particular talk.

As the webinar moved forward, I was blindly vomiting the techy stuff, codes, strategies of getting more clients, science behind marketing etc, at the end I asked for the price that would you give me 8000 Rs and I will change your business.

Guess what happened:

Nobody answered, I again asked for the price, they frankly node it off. It was sooooooooo! embarrassing moment for me. I was feeling so uncomfortable about it, that nobody moved.

Since I was sitting on a chair and was doing it in front of a camera, my legs was really paining, at this condition created a really really huge depression and disaster for me. I then said: OK if you do not want I can leave, they said: "OK!"

I literally went to depression that night, I was feeling sooooo! embarrassed and for next 3 days I could not sleep, I packed up my desk and stop working on my business and was watching TV day and night to change my mind.

Then I realized that everything happens for a reason and the person who is totally responsible for my life and things happen in it is totally myself, so I decided to learn the presentation skills, working on that particular issue day and night, and doing some more messy webinars, finally I perfected the art of selling to masses via webinars and group seminars. I also burnt my boats, because I wanted to take the island. Most of us always create a backup. Entrepreneurs who wanna change the world, have to burn their second options and avoid all those

          R̲ITISH N̲ANCHAHAL

things which breaks their focus from there goal and that is what we call RISK TAKING.

Every good thing in my life happened because there was an entrepreneur that took a risk, who did something that didn't make a lot of sense, to put themselves out there to change everything for somebody else. The thing that makes us entrepreneurs weird, while the majority of the world is trying to get rid of responsibility, entrepreneurs look at something and say, that is a problem, that's my problem, it's not my responsibility but I'm going to take and figure out a way to solve this problem. That's what makes entrepreneurs different.

So I want you guys to understand that right now you may be here at different points in your business, some of you guys are at a high spot in growth mode, you're having fun, some of you guys are in the beginner mode and you're struggling, some of you guys are in between. If you will start taking money as analytics from the starting day, things got worse, you will become money motivated, your impact will never grow. I want you to understand, when you really look at it, say "Look, my business is a calling. I've been called by someone higher, something higher. It's calling me to do this. I am here placed on this earth to serve other people." and when you look at it through that lens, everything else becomes easier.

When you look at it like, "I'm trying to figure out how to make more money for myself." business becomes harder. When you look at it from this lens, life becomes so much easier. There's no way I would have even 5000 people to work with me, if I was trying to make a bunch of money on this. I believe my message so much, that's why I keep talking about it over and over and over and over and over, so I be consistent with it. That's why I am confident and have planned to impact 1 million lives in next 10 years.

Devoted to all non venture startups with no safety nets

Okay, number three, a Funnel Hacker is in control of their destiny. They start without a safety net, venture capital and support. Funnel Hackers need to find their own destiny, they create their own luck, they build their empires, and they change the world. You know as we have, I've told this story a lot of times, as we've been growing a weird company and looking what the next phase, the next step is, my friends always come to me, they're like, "How in the world did you grow a business without any money? It makes no logical sense." I say, "Well, it's the principles we teach all the Funnel Hackers. We use funnels, we practice what we preach, we drink our own fears. We build funnels that grow companies profitably." And that's the power, and gives you guys so much freedom that you don't even understand.

Devoted to all non venture startups with no safety nets

Having no venture capital, it means every single rupee I am investing is coming out of my pocket, that's why we have to think different, we have to think smarter and reverse engineer the system and map down each and every step to our destiny.

So that is our manifesto again on the back. It ends with, "I am a Funnel Hacker, and I'm just one funnel away from my destiny." I got one more thing to talk about before we kind of transition, and this is something we're going to be pushing a lot over the next twelve months. Inside of this entrepreneurial world, I think the message that some of you have been hearing over and over again is wrong. The message of "We need to hustle, hustle, hustle." The message of all these different things that are coming out there. I don't think that's the message of entrepreneurship, not true entrepreneurship.

The message of true entrepreneurship is this, how do we over deliver? And this isn't just in your business, it's in all aspects of your life. It's interesting, I did a podcast about this a little while ago. I talked about 5 lessons learnt from the letters of Jeff Bezoz to his shareholders.

https://qrgo.page.link/azEAD

"As a funnel hacker, we have to harness the power of overdilivery. Jeff bezoz commented about this like

1. As a leader you get visibility, whether that's in front of a national television audience or your local community.
2. Never miss a chance to promote your company or product, but...

3. Practice your delivery. It should feel natural, casual, or like an off the cuff joke. Nobody likes someone who's constantly selling.

Read point 3 carefully again, It shows the human nature that we hate people who are constantly selling and talk to you just for selling, rather than it if somebody changes his message to helping you out, no matter how many papers he would print, no mater how much ink he used to create your documents, but he is doing everything for you to figure out that problem, that adds a unique taste. Amazon is not the symbol of e com because it sells everything, its because it sells everything in a unique approach and it shows you related products, if you are buying a DSLR, it will show you special offer on DSLR covers and Tripods, that means specifically it is caring for your need, that way amazon is selling 3 products at same time as well as it became user friendly and trustworthy for the global audience. Funnel hackers harness the power of overdilivery, they have big visions and goals, so they never care about those sneaky ink and printing costs, but they charge on value that their service is going to add in the consumers' lives.

And this is the thing I want us all thinking about in all aspects of our life. In our relationships with our family, you show up and you're like, "Oh I'm doing the thing, I'm doing the motions." When your child asks for a nice coffee treat, you go and buy extra cookies with coffee, just to get a smile on his face, that's how the love begins and this is the power of overdilivering. Or you coming and saying, "How in this situation with my wife, with my kids, with my spouse, with my whatever it is for you, how do I over deliver in this situation?" How do you over deliver in your business relationships, how do you over deliver in your businesses? As you guys start thinking about that over and over and over again, it's going to change everything for you.

Do you guys when you come to my webinars you saw the little mini world I built here, It became a culture you will see free gifts, charity programme, the energy you get with it and the you will like, "Oh my gosh, Funnel Doc is over delivered.' My goal is to do that in every single interaction. I talked about it with my staff, distant team. Every interaction with someone, it's not like I'm going to do the thing, I'm going to deliver, I'm going to get it done. It's like, no, no, no. I don't want people to get things done. I don't want people to deliver on things. I want everybody to over deliver. And this is my message for the next year. How do we over deliver in all situations? So are you guys okay if we over deliver this opportunity for you. You okay with that? Alright, okay, for that some of you might say that you're an entrepreneur by birth, but because you are here, you guys are Funnel Hackers by choice. That's what it means to be a Funnel Hacker.

RITISH NANCHAHAL

SOLO SHORTCUTS

Coming to this part of the book, I want to talk about shortcuts.

Okay so, I don't know, if you follow me on Instagram (@hackritish)

https://www.Instagram.com/hackritish

you've probably seen the pieces of it, but I've been slightly cracking over the last 5 or 6 weeks because the load has been heavy, like insanely heavy. In fact, 2 months ago I made a list of all the stuff I have to do and I was just like, 'I don't think this is possible." And couple of nights I couldn't sleep, I wake up until like 4 or 5 in the morning because I stressed about it. Which then made it worse because the next day I couldn't even function, I was tired and losing days and it was just like, ugh. The stress was depressing me, but daily chores was pushing me to do the work, my exams are near, I was also stressed about that, and the worst heating sun, hottest summers in my life, we have just shifted so the coolers and ac were not yet taken to new location, ugh it was the horrific climatic experience that you can ever imagine, everything was tending me to feel inefficient and tired.

End of the day I was not able to complete anything, even after remaining busy for 18 hours. This lead to health issue, typhoid and Platelets drainage.

Anyway, but I'm at the end. I'm at the last step. As soon my exams will end I'm going to be on vacation for like 2 weeks with nature and just unplug and (breathes deeply) catching a breath of fresh air. But it's been heavy. And it's interesting because 3 days ago, well, my cousin (Ramninder) came to meet me from Banglore, which made me feel a little tense free and happy, with the family.

So it's like, I hate, I don't want to ever be the person who misses the party because of work. I have missed a lot enjoyment in my learning phase, but our mind needs a change somewhere in life, when routine gets non-tolerable. So I'm like, 'I have to be part of the party."

So sleep is like, basically I'm like, 'I gotta get rid of something, the only thing I can get rid of is sleep. I'm not getting rid of fun, I'm not getting rid of family, I'm not getting rid of projects. I'm going to pull out sleep and just get rid of it." which you can't do for too long.

Our mind is so resilient that it can learn anything. We all have 24 hours to spend, so getting no time for the tasks you want to do but cannot do is the worst excuse, the more we learn to prioritize, the more efficiently we will grow. Even I am not sure, how I started writing this book and even not sure, what I will write in next chapters, but its my priority to end half chapter a day, so that I can complete the whole tasks, including marketing, publishing and printing before end of 2 months.

Anyway, now it's Sunday so I got only 2 weeks left for me to go and complete whole organic chemistry and modern physics revision that I am left with, since the exam are going to start in less than 3 weeks. I have to get those all done, then plus I have a 5 day event, which is a virtual event, on lead capturing secrets, 5 day lead challenge, going to do as soon the exams will be over, which means I'm the only one there speaking. So I've got a dozen or so presentations or so that I'm working on there, needless to say it is a lot. The burden is heavy. But the good news is it's almost the end. The end of this week I'm going to be able to unplug and just be like, huh (breathes).

So what I want to talk about though, is shortcuts. Because in the process of this, as I'm moving

    RITISH NANCHAHAL

forward as fast as I can to get all these things done, I have to look for shortcuts, because there's no way to get everything done. It's impossible. So you have to look for shortcuts.

So one of the nice things that I like about this whole, I don't know maybe it's bad, but for me, I try to get everything, I don't pre.....not that I don't pre-plan or prioritize, but everything is good when its done in limit, I just, it's like, just in time production. Like, everything will get done just in time. It doesn't get done early ever. It never has in my entire life. I never got homework done until the minute it was due. I never got projects done, because if it's like, if I plan it too far in advance then I have all this time to think, and then, I don't know, the greatness comes when you're under pressure and stressed, and you start discovering these shortcuts.

So yesterday, we got back from the factory outlets, I'm sitting there, it's like 10 o'clock, almost 10 o'clock at night, I'm about to start working on my portfolio funnels again. I'm just like, "I'm not going to get this done in time." And I'm thinking, "how can I shortcut this? How can I shorten this?" I'm looking for the shortcut right. And then it appeared. And the shortcut in this situation was, "Who's service, who's content, who's process could I reverse engineer with to shortcut what I'm doing?"

And all the sudden I was like, "Oh my gosh." There was a client's portfolio funnel that I have to create this week, I mean realistically it would take about less than a hour to create, but can take about a week to plan, the whole thing since its the first client that asked for a funnel that tells audience about himself (portfolio). And it would have been good, but I don't know if it could have been great. And I was like, "Oh my gosh, there's someone on the glove who creates a portfolio funnel that's really great. Can I shortcut?

So I jumped to google and found some of the portfolio funnels that are driving much traffic to the creator's products and services, I called my friends I'm like, "Hey, I need a quick favor. Would you be willing to spend 15 minutes to do a quick survey and figure out the key elements of these successful portfolio funnels that I am sending to you and tell me what are the most appealing parts of it to you as a customer of it?" and within about 1 hour I figured out a doodle and a structure and today I'm using the same doodle to create a lot of portfolio funnels that really make money. These are the examples of portfolio funnels I got inspired from:-

And what's crazy is it just shortcutted me. I just bought myself a week back that I would have had to figure out somewhere, like on the boat in sea with no shore and no compass or map . That wouldn't have worked. Anyway, but I brought myself a week back. And the reality is that funnel was so much better than what I had created. Like it's already, a finished product "This is way better than what I would have done." That portfolio funnel was so much more detail oriented and everything is more thought through. But it was just

  RITISH **N**ANCHAHAL

a shortcut. It was a shortcut that saved me worth of time, effort and energy it saved me so much stress, and anxiety, and then it actually turned out better than if I would have done it myself.

So it got me thinking like, where else can I shortcut things? I'm looking at now everything I'm doing right now in this window. I'm like, what can I not do? What can I give someone else? What's the things? Where can I shortcut things? I started teaching this concept but you know better than I do and and I'm speeding up my process. This is how I made the art of funnel sketching the tactics so tangible. I have already told you that we are funnel hackers and we create revolutions with no sponsorship and venture capital, so rather than investing too much, time effort, energy and feed backs to create something from zero, its more effective to take your inspiration of something that already working, being a pioneer and trying everything in your business will teach you that there are millions of wrong ways to do the same job, but only the one way to do it right. Remember pioneers always have arrows in there back. That's why I harness the power of reverse engineering and I call it FUNNEL CLONING.

Anyway, I want to share this because I had this conversation with Varinder who, those who don't know Varinder, he's my cousin and, he's the dude who pushed me to do what I am doing today. He's a genius. Literally the smartest person I've ever met. And founder of businesses like socioninja, and CMO at Executive Advantage. Don't tell him that because his head will get bigger. No, he's like literally the smartest person I've ever met in my life.

And it's funny because we were talking about him and other developers and things like that, and he said, he told me, "The thing that makes me the best of business creators is because I'm so lazy." I'm like, "What? Dude you are not lazy. You are the hardest worker." He's like, "I know I'm a hard worker," but he's like, "The reason why I'm such a good entrepreneur and I get things done so fast is because I look at everything and I'm like, oh I can do this and there's a 6 month version and I could do this and it could get done in 6 months. But is there a way I can get this done in 2 days instead?" And that's the thought he always looks at. "Instead of me building the whole business the whole thing from scratch, I joint venture or I borrow this here, and then get these libraries..." I don't know, this is all What business tycoons do, but what I do, I copy there lifestyle, I follow there routines, habits, I read there books, I learn from their courses and content, that made me boosting the process of business creation.

And it's funny because he's trained me and to some extent, my family start thinking that way. In fact, 'When you look at problem you're like, okay this is going to take me 6 months. you will take 6, or most probably, more than 6 months. But when you change your attitude, the way you handle the situation, things change, the way that you have never thought of before.

So I want you to start looking at your projects that way, and a lot of times there's shortcut. A lot of times there's a way you could do something faster. You could be licensing someone's product, you hiring somebody. It could be like a million different things, but what's the shortcut you can do today that gets you there faster?

So I wanted to share that today because Reverse engineering the thought of Varinder, I saved myself at least 5 years worth of work, made the product better, and everyone's happy. Getting all this credibility because he was there to direct me on a

  RITISH | **NANCHAHAL**

path when I was dreaming. I got to save myself time and effort. Usually Small things give big results, these cannot be said as coincidences, great stories do not happen by chance, they are created, Varinder helped me to start my own business, now the 1 life he has impacted, not only change my way, but also its a huge boost to his confidence and self proud. I can pay him back the money and effort, he invested on me, but I can never payback that feeling. So I have decided, as soon I will take myself on the exponential graph too, rather than buying assets or a new car for myself at the beginning, I would much prefer to help some other children of that time to grow there businesses and stand up strong on there feet.

So there you go, there's the thought for today I wanted to drop on you as you're doing your projects and figuring out what is the shortcut. Putting your Funnel Hacker on and figuring out the shortcut. With that said, thank you guys so much for everything and hopefully you're moving forward on your projects and getting back to changing the world in your own little way. And with that said, I will see you in next chapter...

AGE IS JUST A NUMBER

> "Age is just a number that defines how long you've lived, but don't let it define how you live."
> Emily Shai

I watched a Mini film On funnel hackers TV presenting a 11 year old funnel hacker Emily Shai and Caleb Maddix.

Emily Shai, at time of movie recording 11 years old and she started a business called Emily sleepovers to raise money and wrote a book called 5 steps to perfect sleepovers in just 1 month and selling it for 15$ each. With this amazing enthusiasm and simple but consistent approach to new book buyers, she raised 20,000$. Its almost 15 lacs.

I have seen there FB lives, the stuff they are doing online and impacting lives of people at this younger age. Emily told that her business got the born fire when she wanted to buy a phone at age 10, so she asked about money to her dad. Her dad being a very practical man, replied her that if you really wanna buy a phone for yourself, go and start a business and raise money for it.

That's how she made the decision that she gonna write a book. not being a teen, but more thinking as a adult, I really like the way her father tackled the situation and asked her daughter to start a business, we have seen many people flying to other countries on loans and then doing odd jobs there, but he became an example for other fathers too that pushing your kids to business world, not only will make there innovation come out , it will make them self independent and boost their confidence. Also they will learn to take care of the stuff they will buy from there money and they will feel its true value.

Both Caleb and Emily made a funnel, on giving a free workshop to people on topic AGE IS JUST A NUMBER. They created a free hover-board giveaway

Caleb Maddix told that how he was having a habit of doing consistent fb lives from young age. He posted a video with topic WHY YOU ARE POOR at early teenage. Can you believe it, it gone viral, but the comments was really depressing. He told in the session that People were really aggressive and against that nerdy kid who is teaching others WHY YOU ARE POOR?

After reading 11 comments, he felt nearly died on 12; there was written that Caleb you must attempt suicide, the world will be a happier place. Then he read the next comment, it was a thank you message from a lady telling him the story that how her little child was going to attempt suicide, he was depressed from his low grades, low confidence and no friends, but this little video made him mentally strong and confident to do not care what others say and do a startup. His little video not only saved a life, but also induced life in a living dead. That's what I loved the most. Impacting one live out of 10 can even create a great change in the lives, and that's the Attitude of funnelhackers

I really appreciate these young minds, when others of there age were watching Netflix and chill, they were doing startups and build. At mine pre teen age I was not having access to internet and this wordily wisdom, so I started to give tuition to the students of younger age, in 2 years that little tuition centre changed that tuition centre changed to a leading institute, THE LEARNING HUB, that's how I did my first startup, In my crisis time, the time when my father met a road accident and got stitches on head, and my mother recovering from her liver surgery, that particular THE LEARNING HUB, helped me to cover all expenses of house for strict 8 months (till my father and mother rejoined on work). That's how a hobby of teaching that I got from doing mimicry of my teachers lead to a lifeline in hard times.

My target for this year is to impact more than 50000 people and especially children to create a business using funnels that will gift them their dream life in reality. I want they should get the respect and abundance that they deserve.

I learnt from a 3 day live conference: There are no good or bad people, there are no calm and aggressive people, we are humans, everything is in our inside. In room there is nobody gentry than us, also nobody is more tyrannical than us. We can be whatever we want. We can create whatever we want. There are no barriers. Age is also not a barrier.

With mine experience, Emily's story and Caleb's startup, I wanna put your eyesight on the fact that age really does not matter. No matter you are in your early 11-12 years, or you are in your late 90, you can still impact that world, and that's what the mission of a funnel hacker is. Its like avengers endgame, In funnel hackers endgame "We are going to impact the world till last sigh"

RITISH NANCHAHAL

THE POWER TO PIVOT

What's up, everybody. This is Ritish Nanchahal. I want to go a little Tony Robbins on you if you're okay with that. We've been dealt with some of the hardest phases in history in last year. The education, jobs, market was totally crashed. We passed the most lonely phase of our life, when there was even danger from loving ones. Covid-19 not only shifted the socioeconomic, but also it made us mentally depressed and broken. Many people lost hope, But there was a part of the world, who was thriving in online industry. The you-tubers with channels from last 5 years and having 500k subscribers, suddenly passed 4.85M in lockdown period. The E advertising market was on height. It was the golden period for many Businesses and startups that gone viral and on exponential profits in just some months. They were not surviving, they were thriving. One of the personality that I found was growing consistently was the Tony Robbins.

The one thing that I watched a recording on his UPW and learnt from it the most it's interesting. It's this thing that I learned from Tony Robbins very first time. I didn't know that recording was how much old. It was over 10, maybe 12, probably 12 years ago. It was the year when Jim Rowan, the actual mentor of Tony Robbins passes away 3 days before the event.

PIVOTING IS THE ONLY WAY TO YOUR FULL POTENTIAL

Tony starts talking about his mentor who just passed away. And he talks about how obviously how sad it was for them. And then he started talking about this concept and he expounded on it at other events. He talked about the meaning that we attach to things. And it was interesting because so many of us experienced the same things, But the meaning that we attach to things is how we end up feeling and how we cope with things. Right? And so, for example, he said, when Jim Rowan first passed away, his first year, the first initial news and your mind automatically attaches a meaning to it, right? By default, the meaning he got was like, "Oh my gosh, my mentor died. This is so sad. Like I wish I could have talked to him. I wish..." And all these things. And this was meaning is that this thing is so sad and so hard. And it's because of it, it was hard.

 RITISH **N**ANCHAHAL

He's like, for the first couple of days, I struggled, I was really struggling, but he's like, as I stopped and I was able to sit back, I started noticing like, what was the meaning that I put to this? Like the, his death and like the meeting was man, I wasn't ready for him to go. You know, it was too early. All these things like, that was the meeting that my, that my brain by default attaches.

And because I was able to step away and become conscious of meaning that attached. I was able to think about well, what meaning would I like to attach to this event? I can change the meaning. And so he sat back and he said, "I'm going to change the meaning." And instead of saying, "This is such a horrible thing. I'm like going to change the meaning. It means like, man, I'm so grateful for the time I had with him. I'm so grateful things I learned from him, such an amazing man." And he lived such a great life, like how amazing it was. And so he shifted the meeting. "When I shifted the meaning, like the feeling was different. And I went from being sad to being like, man, this is such a, I was so grateful for this person."

When I reach new people and they came to know that the reason why I prefer funnels over websites is that I make funnels for others, They think, Shh!

this guy gonna approach to sell me his services, But when I show them the fact that how it is changing the lives of customers by saving time and getting what they wanted, as well as the sellers to get there message out to the world and impacting thousands of lives, suddenly their thoughts changes to; This person is like a Torch bearer and so much embedded in clients' results rather than money, I should work with him.

And again this is just a tiny little shift, but so powerful. And as I've been experiencing dealing with things over the last little while, I've been trying to be more conscious of what things in my brain... What's the meaning that my brain attaches by default when an experience happens. And typically when it's a sad or a tragic or a hard experience, your brain defaults to link it with the worst thing, right?

Rather than thinking like "I am sick," we can change the meaning to "I am not well," Its better to say "will meet soon" than "goodbye," Its worthy to say "I am Not rich rather than saying I am poor" and soo many examples we can use here. And if you can learn how, to step back from the initial, what your brain quickly labels something on, you can shift things, right?

  RITISH | NANCHAHAL

The things that evolve, can only retain, We have seen in our science book that the beetles that became green with time, was able to hide themselves from crows and vultures, whereas red beetles gone wiped off by nature. As the dotcom bubble burst in 2003, only those companies survives, that evolved and was ready to evolve all the time. Now its the end of the website era, and the companies who pivoted to funnels are secured from the upcoming bubble burst.

Moving back to Tony's UPW. As the dates were announces, the people booked their seats for UPW Last year, Suddenly, BOOM!, lockdown, pack-up, closed. But Tony mastered the art of Pivoting. He suddenly changed the Location to Australia, in next week, Unfortunately, Australia was closed, flights were off. It became a stress on his team that UPW will not happen this year and we have to pay back all the tickets that we have charged to the attendees. But this was something Not digest-able to Tony Robbins. Rather than realizing, that they cannot do UPW, he pivoted his beliefs to Not doing UPW In a Big Stadium or Setup, Suddenly he got an idea to do it virtually, and without wasting time he started to build a big studio with a giant circular screen on which he can see the faces of thousands of attendees and then can feel the same energy. He contacted to the CEO of Zoom and got a on demand version of zoom for thousands of attendees for his event specially. And this is how, he was able to successfully do the UPW as well as world's summit even in hardship.

And now you apply different meaning. And it's like, "Oh." And I know for me, like man, especially social media and all social media triggers all of us, right. Where you see something, you see somebody post something and all the triggers start happening and you start firing your brain. You want to like, duh, unleash your wrath upon them in the comments. And what I've been trying to do really quickly is stop and looking and saying, "Okay, I'm going to assume that this person has really good intentions when they're posting. I may not agree with it but I do agree that most people do things out of good intentions, even if I feel they're misguided or whatever, but they have good intentions." Right? I believe politically, people on the left and the right and in the middle and all sorts of all that they say, everyone's acting out of good intentions.

Personally I never forward any massage or thought I get on my whattsap, I have seen similar happening to my father that When he sent a post to my uncle that was having a fact based on reality, but to my uncle it looks like a personally did comment and they were not happy with that.

People are all doing what they think is right. Even though I think some people are completely wrong, it doesn't matter. They think I'm completely wrong. Right. And so it's like when they post something, I have the meaning of like, "Oh, they're evil, they're bad." Like that's the initial default that has come back saying, "Wait, wait." Instead, what if I attach the meaning that person has the good intentions. And I may not agree with them, but they're doing the best based on what they think is right. And then we see, it's like how people parent, how people vote, how people, all these things. And it's tough because we want to fight. We want to be right. What I've been trying to do a step back and not default comment, not default fight back, but instead come back, say, okay, the meaning attached to that person's comment, it's not that they're dumb or they're wrong or they're whatever. It's just like, that person thinks that they're doing what's best for them. They have good intentions. I love them for the fact that they're doing their best based on the knowledge they have.

And it's hard. I'm going to tell you, it's hard. I'm sure all you guys struggle with that. But for me, it's what I'm trying to do for a lot of reasons. One is it's keeping my sanity on somethings. Number two, it's helping me to be happier through these hard times. Right. Something tragic and horrible happens, it's okay, there's different meanings we can attach to this. It's not fair. It's why did it have to happen? Why did we... All these things or can make man what's the blessing, what's the shift? What's the thing we can change. And so I know it's not an easy thing. This is not something that's going to be like, Oh cool. I'll just start applying different meanings by default. But I do promise you that in most situations, our brains will slap the worst possible meaning on every situation.

And if we can look at that and stop and pause and become conscious of it and step back and say, "Okay, I'm going to choose a different meaning. This is the meaning I'm going to attach instead." Is that this person confused, that commented on me because they didn't know who I was. They thought I was the wrong person, or they didn't understand the situation. Let me step back instead of punching them back and escalating this thing into a blood bath, which is actually fun. I'm just kidding. Instead is come back and say, "Well, okay, they attached the wrong me. That's why they did this thing. Let me try to help them understand."

I didn't, and coming back, we have an argument, I wasn't trying to be rude. This is the meaning that I attach to this and this is the reason, and this is why. Anyway, I hope that helps.

I learnt from Sam ovens that Most of the conflicts occur because everybody in this world Thinks that the frontier should think, how I thinks. in arguments, All of us try to make others respect our authority, respect our decisions and respect our opinions, when the tuning does not match, aggression, disputes and conflict occurs, Right?

Remember that your brain is going to slap a meaning on it. By default, it's going to be the worst possible one that's going to cause you to want to fight or flight or whatever that thing is. It's like your job to consciously stop and pick the meaning, that serves you the most, not the one that's going to cause the most turmoil in your life. And when you shift the meaning, it's just shifts the energy, it shifts the focus, and it can change your destiny.

Our thoughts create our beliefs, our belief create our actions, our action give results, result create similar feedbacks (environmental responses) and hence it becomes our reality.

UNIT:-2

(FUNNELOLOGY)

MY FIRST SUCCESSFUL FUNNEL

What's up everybody, this is Ritish Nanchahal and in this part of this book I am going to uncover my secret funnel strategy that makes me 36000 Rs every single month with just a simple 7 day recorded training. The funnel that was totally garbage at the time when it was launched, and evolved slowly and I kept on rewiring its framework and stuff and finally it reached a position where it is making 1200rs per day. Working 24/7. Like a passionate salesman that never give excuses, never off at weekends and never asks for raises even. It works consistently and effortlessly.

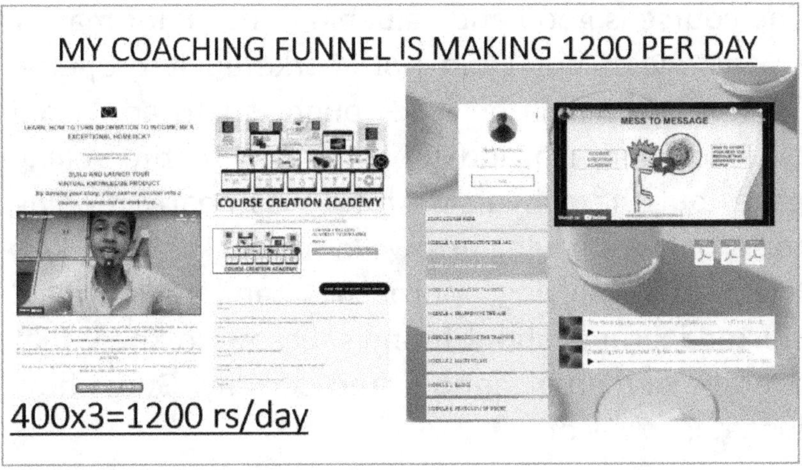

Its about this passed June 2020, when I started to work on course creation academy program. My intention of this program was to help school students to find a idea from mess of their thoughts and then convert that set of knowledge to a proper online course in just 7 days.

The message, the idea was powerful, but it does not means that if you have the best recipe, you will succeed. The marketing plays a very important role. Starbucks do not have the best coffee in the world. Someone's grandma may have it, but she never thought of it as a business level and did not marketed it. The solution to a problem that is marketed properly and became well known to its potential audience, succeed.

The course is good and valuable, it does not matter to the most, but I did not marketed it properly. Then when I realized it, I bought some ads, I did organic approach and driven traffic to the selling page, but the conversion ratio was nearly tending to zero. I was having arrows in my back, since I was trying and applying approaches randomly. Then I started learning about funnels. I came to know that average human attention time per day. Guess how long it is? 7 seconds!

    RITISH | NANCHAHAL

Due to the 7 seconds time limit, our traditional websites are blocking visitors to buy stuff from us and become our regular customers.

Websites are pretty but pointless, moreover they are cluttered and confusing, that's why their end is near. The another bubble is going to burst very soon. Then I created a sales funnel that grab people's attention and then lead them through a process, so that every second that is passing of watching the site, it provides them enough knowledge about product and motivation of buying, so that they checkout and BOOM!! Customer acquired!

Today we live in a internet world. Everyday ads, trackers, pop-ups are covering us and trying us to sell something. Even in the offline markets, banners, leaflets, TV ads are trying to sell us something, so it became our nature to ignore them all, right?

As a customer we know it, but as a seller we miss this point. We feel, something that we created, something that is very close to our heart, that we are trying to sell gonna effect lives, so every visitor of our site, should pay same attention and respect to it, right?

Ritish Nanchahal

But its not the truth, nobody cares the effort, energy you invested, no body actually knows it's value, that's why, the problem with them and their business, these days, that's why confusion, loose temper and panic occurs.

If I ask somebody about, what's the issue of your financial crisis, He will say, its problem with my business, when I asked what problem, he replied Less profits. But less money is nothing but another name of financial crisis, its not the issue, its the issue in sales funnel. Consequences can be like less site traffic, so we need lead funnels. It can be less conversion ratio, so we need to care about 7 indigents of funnels to create buying urgency. It can be the reason your site is not delivering the answer to the questions occurring in mind of the potential customers. It maybe lot of distractions on your site, it can be anything like that, but all of them represent problems with the sales funnel, right?

I was in sort of hopelessness at the time when my coursecreationacademy.co.in was not working well. So I recreated the sales page from scratch. I still have that old page. When the registered users will visit the site to start learning, they will see an article, that was the old sales page, it give you a tons of info, but it becomes boring and it gives a vague idea, I kept that page still to show others the difference between a common sales website approach and a funnel approach. This link now redirects you to a sales page where it shows my motivation, idea, what you will get if you invest today, also up-sells and down-sells help me to sell more things at the same time.

coursecreationacademy.co.in

Let me show you how it is

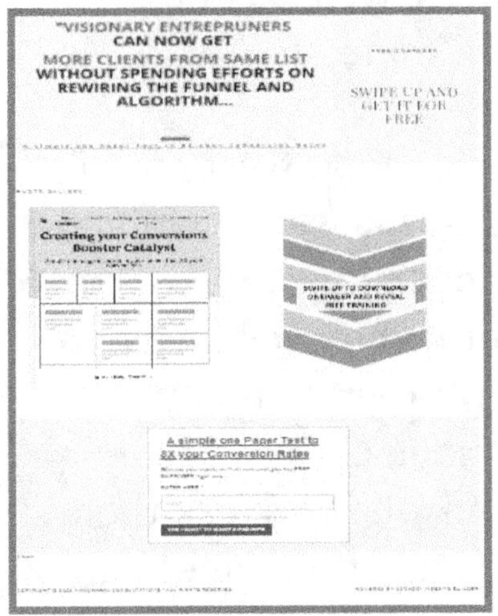

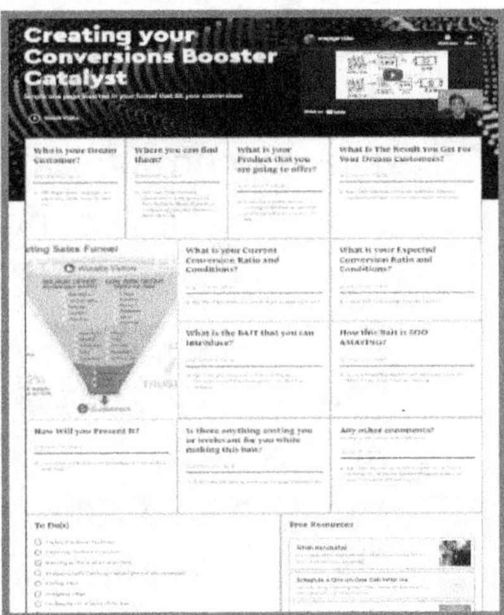

THIS ONE PAGE FUNNEL ACTS LIKE A SALES REPRESENTATIVE

Devoted to all non venture startups with no safety nets

1. At start, it knows very well that the visitor do not wanna buy anything, so it shows the vision and message.

2. The people who are interested in similar vision and the people with whom that message resonated, only will move forward, as they swipe down, there is a video of mine telling them about my success, my story and similar opportunity that I am going to give them through this course. putting my own video, wins their trust as well as the best salesperson that can sell mine stuff is I , Me and Myself.

3. The percentage of people I won trust of, will now scroll again, now they will see my funnel representing the opportunity and telling them what they will get if they will invest in course creation academy program today.

4. in next section, till this piece a weird bug came to customer's mind when we ask them about investment, some other lines are motivating them, enthusiasing them to invest and telling them that this can be a life changing moment for their life.

5. The price scheme that I used is called the Short Note Technique, I learnt it from Dan Kennedy, he says till the time you have told everything about your product. Dan Kennedy

said that as you move forward, your mind erases the backward. Telling large number of advantages and offers to your customer one by one, customer's mind is going to miss or erase some of those from memory at point when they gonna click the checkout button, so writing all the offers and advantages in tabular or list form can be advantageous, it then follows a stack approach, that boosts up the sales and make people jump from seats in seminars to buy from you just like popcorn pop in pan.

6. Putting the checkout button after each step is strategic, the more availability of checkout buttons, more will be the chances of transaction and getting profited.

So that's the portion of a simple one page sales funnel that make me 1200 Rs per day consistently (on an average). I always say, the more you will be in, the more you dive deeper into this concept, the more you gonna understand the concept better. The first step is to read this book thoroughly. Read one chapter, apply it, read it, apply it. That's how you will perfect your funnel process. After completing this book, try to figure out parables and funnel problems in your website or non working funnels. Figure it out on your behalf, for deep understanding or one on one personal guidance, you can go through the link below, and then we both (together) can analyse your funnel and level it up. Remember; this session will be <u>free of cost</u> as promised. I will see you then...

https://calendly.com/ritishnanchahal

THE VALUE LADDER

"What is your strategy", I asked on a call, and suddenly TEEEEE.....

Ah! He cut my phone. Hello-hello!! (then no answers)

What's up everybody, the sun is up, the cool breeze of this morning enforced me to write this chapter right now. Those were the some of first words I spoke to a visa consultant, his number I found from internet and he cut my phone.

I wanna tell you the incident of my first sales call that I ever made and it was so horrible. I still have its recording somewhere in my backup drives and it makes me feel that how this nerd can ever make money? Just kidding, but seriously that call was not ever appreciable, and in case if my mentors were present in front of me that time, they gonna beat me off with their shoes.

Morning time, I created a list of potential customers to call and wrote their contact details one by one.

I called one of them and our conversation like that

                    RITISH **N**ANCHAHAL

Me:-"Hello! What's up? Am I talking to Mr......................?"

His Team:-"yes good morning, we are from his team, how can we help you?"

"Just forward this call to your director, I want to talk him personally"

"Sure, just wait for 2 minutes, and I am forwarding this call to him."

Him,: "Yes, who's this?"

"Good morning sir, how are you doing"

"great, who are you and the reason you called?"

"Actually I found your contact on internet and I found you are teaching ielts to a lot students, but I was curious to know, why there were no google ads working out there."

"I did not understand"

"actually I help businesses like you to grow via using google and fb ads, Your competitors are spending on ads, why you don't?"

    RITISH **N**ANCHAHAL

"We use them occasionally, why you are Calling to us?"

"It's simple you pay me money, I will give you traffic"

"Why should I trust you?"

"Oh! I have a different paradigm, I am success motivated person, I give you results and then results will speak for themselves."

"Let me contact you tomorrow"

"Yes sure, I have listed your number and I will reach you tomorrow and discuss further details."

Tee...... (Phone cut)

That day passes, other day passed, day after day passed, neither he called back, nor he picked up my phone. Still I was feeling, "poor guy! he missed a great opportunity." "Why he not contacted me back?"

Similarly I sent mails to tons of people I found a website providing database of contact information, I was wow!!!!!!! Without thinking anything I invested in it and downloaded a list of almost

10000 people of my niche and I started to send mails to them in pack of 50 addresses one time. I became a goat person, that do meh! meh! meh! and keep pushing my services and vomiting my knowledge in those early mails, Since I did it in time of 4g internet, so it took less than 5 minutes to be sent. I enabled the email tracking, I found most of the email addressed were not found, they were totally waste, and some of those were working. But bad feeling arises when nobody of those were replying me and I was not getting any talk moving further. 3 days after doing same task consistently, I got a mail, literally I got a mail, and when I opened that, UGH!, It was mail from Email security services and the writer of the mail was shouting on me, since I got spam reports on my email addresses more than I can even imagine in last 3 days. Then I understood why there are no more blue ticks in tracker, when I sent 2nd mail to those same addresses. I got penalized and I lost my professional email that day. That was kind of my SPAM STORY. That passed, I committed to never buy databases like that.

I was in state of panic, I thought of quitting that time, I asked the reason why I am not getting any clients in a social media post and I got a great answer from a entrepreneur from Boise, Idaho

He told me, your business is like your girlfriend, Do you have one?

I said "no"

"Why?"

"I am INTJ personality, never understand that kind of stuff."

"Ok! then you can understand better the logic.

The more time you give to it, the more interest you will take in it, the more love and care it will pay you back and taking the same example tell me If you wanna propose her, how you will approach?"

"First I will make her a good friend, care her, like she expects, help her in usual tasks when she needed. Make her feel comfort with me."

"Exactly! Ultimately you are trying to get into a momentum with her, right?

"Yeah! Kind of, kinda momentum with her, right."

"Think of going to a random girl and chatting like you are a beautiful girl, I am a handsome boy, let us get married."

"I don't want her to beat me with her heals."

"Exactly, 99% she will call you crazy and become angry, 1% , exceptional cases, if she agree?"

"Then I will call her crazy."

"Absolutely! But the same thing you are doing with your business, you meet new people, rather than getting into a momentum you are throwing your offers and services that hits them like bricks."

Got it! I understood, yeah! I am doing the same mistake again and again, the problem is neither with me, nor my business, its with the approach I am taking again and again.

"Exactly, nobody likes Sudden changes and decisions specially in case of money investments"

"Deep meaning, thank you for giving me this lesson, I heartily appreciate it."

"It's OK, no worries, bye!"

"Bye, good day."

By the way, I learn something from this conversation that is harnessing the power of value ladder and stuff. Then I started noticing same pattern in the world's variety of businesses.

Why Ice Cream Vendor have a section for tasting the flavors for free?

Why Doctor always do a common healthcare checkup with minimal appointment fee, before diagnosis?

Why people going for free health care checkups loose bunch of grands in paid checkups after they get diagnosed once for free?

Why I invested more than 3000 on my bike's frame, when my early decision was to just change the break leathers?

Everything was giving me same answer, POWER OF GETTING INTO MOMENTUM MAKES US EASY TO LOOSE MONEY AND MAKES BUSINESSES MAKE MONEY. THE POWER OF VALUE LADDER.

We can call value ladder as a step by step approach to increase the efficiency of results and impact in customer's life as well as increase the level of profits.

As the leathers of my bike were changed, I was getting great grip on my speed control, Because I had received value, I naturally wanted to move forward and get additional value from mechanic.

then I invested some grands to clean the filters , change the oils. He then found another way that he could provide value to me—the engine—and again, I naturally took him up on that offer as well. Now, for many mechanics, they make the most money and provide the most value for their customers by offering full customization. Luckily, I didn't need any restoration or customization on that visit, or I could have been out 30,000 Rs or more. On my way out the door, the lady on reception scheduled me for another appointment six months later, adding me to their "continuity" program. Continuity is where you continue paying on a weekly, monthly, or yearly basis until you decide to cancel. and the team of mechanics will keep taking care of your vehicle. This company had a perfectly executed Value ladder.

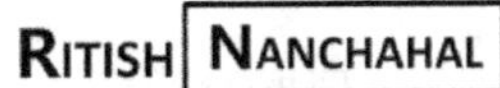

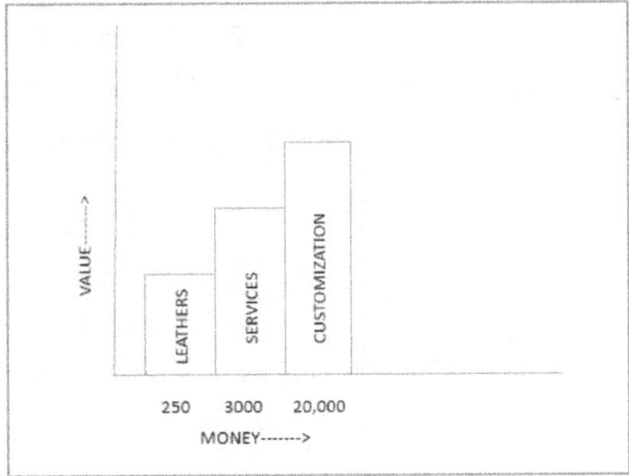

One of the first things I explain to people when I start working with them is the concept of a Value Ladder, and it's the first thing you have to build out before you can start working on any sales funnel. Let us see value ladder of that restoration company as an example. If you look at how we structure it, you'll see that on the left hand axis we have value, and on the bottom axis we show the price.

Now, on the top right hand corner of this graph, you'll see the customization. This is where you want to take your client. This is where you can provide them the most value— and also charge them the most.

For my company, it's going into your business to build out your sales funnels, set up your back-end systems, and generate leads for you. Currently I have services charging from 5000rs to 1 lac Rs, where 1lac+10% profits till 10lacs one is the highest peak of the value ladder. This is the most premium one but here I can provide the best value and it give me energy to give my best

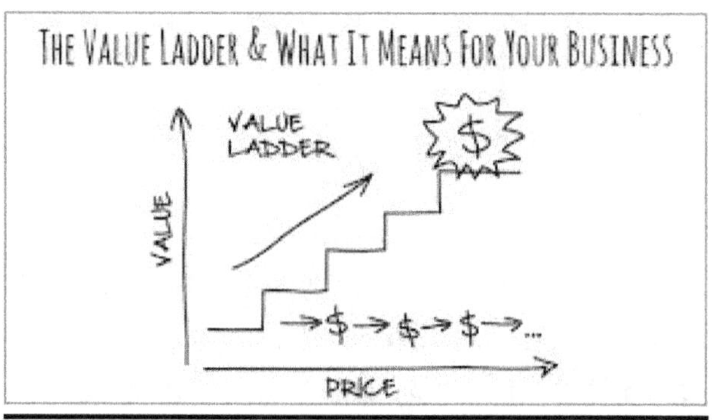

You can use this same model to design your own Value Ladder for your business.

Now, ideally we would like to sell everyone our best thing, right? You want to serve your customers in the highest way possible. But the sad truth is that if I were to walk up to you on the street and say, "Give me 10 lac, and I'll help you to grow your company," you would either laugh in my face or run away, thinking I was insane.

Why is that? It's because we just met, and so far, I haven't provided you any value. But if you came to my website and saw that I was giving away a free course on converting your passion and skill to a information product and launch your virtual brand online and all you had to do was cover the Rs 500 shipping, do you think that you'd order it?

If you're in my target audience you would—because the price is low, and you have a chance to receive some value in a non-threatening way, allowing you to see if you like the experience. Just like I did with the mechanic. Now, if you order that course from me and receive value from it, you will naturally want more. You'll want to ascend my Value Ladder and see if there are other ways I can provide value for you.

You may buy one of my home study courses or attend one of my live events. If you receive value from that, then you may decide to sign up for my personal one on one training program, or maybe my 5 lac Rs Inner Circle program. And if I provide awesome value there, then you will naturally want to keep ascending ... and THAT is how I sell my high ticket package. We provide insane amounts of value at each step of our Value Ladder, so our clients naturally want to ascend, get more value, and pay us more money.

Oh yeah, and just like the mechanic, no Value Ladder is complete without a good continuity program. There are many ways to structure your continuity program. It could be organized around software, membership sites, or ongoing coaching, but it should be something you can bill for each month. That residual income will become the lifeblood of your business. Win-Win.

HOW TO CREATE YOUR VALUE LADDER BUSINESS BLUEPRINT IF YOU DO NOT HAVE ASCENDING CHAIN OF PRODUCTS?

Now I'm aware that everyone reading this has a different type of company. At this point, you're probably trying to figure out how the Value ladder applies to your business. I want to share with you a story that will show you how we were able to create a Value Ladder for a business that doesn't seem to have any type of ascending products or services.

Let me tell you mine own story of value ladder. At startup I was ready to help coaches with their websites and fb ads. But it was very difficult to find people and then more harder to sell services to them, to create a value ladder, I written some blogs, I created a podcast, and then put some episodes and shared some value consistently on it and the people who visited my podcast, a percentage of them move forward and visit my website, a ratio of them enroll in my course creation academy program and then they move forward on my extended value ladder to get more value for me till my high ticket programme. This is how, not only I get automated sales and new customers, but also I can diversify those people into groups of regular, high paying etc clients.

You might be selling a book right now on the front-end and have no idea how to build up a back-end Value Ladder. Well, what other value can you provide to people? Can you be more hands-on with them? Can you offer more personal attention? Can you provide ancillary services or physical products that enhance your primary offer? My very first information product was a DVD on class 10th full syllabus revision in one shot lectures. (And that just goes to show you can sell anything online!).

But I figured out how to build a Value Ladder by also selling "Do It Yourself" plans and physical coaching to our customers. The Value Ladder is the key to building your marketing funnels and mastering everything else I'm going to teach you in this book. This system does not work if all you have is one thing—like a book or an adjustment. You need to be able to build out a full Value Ladder.

     RITISH NANCHAHAL

Most businesses I look at have one or two pieces of the ladder, but they rarely have all four. Once we add in the missing pieces, the business can start to expand dramatically. There's no end to the level of back-end services and experiences you can add. If you keep providing more and more value, people will spend more and more money to keep working with you.

A percentage of your audience will always want to pay you the premium to get more value. The only limit to your value offerings is your imagination. Keep thinking of higher and higher levels of service, and you can keep charging more and more money. There's always something else you can offer.

WHAT IF I DON'T HAVE A VALUE LADDER? Often times, it's hard for companies to figure out how to add more offers to their Value Ladders. Typically, the process is very easy for someone selling information products because that ascension path has already been created and proven in thousands of different information-based companies. But what if you're selling something else? What if you offer physical products, e commerce, B2B services, or professional services where the path isn't quite as clear? Sometimes it takes a little thought and creativity. If you already have a product or a service that you sell in the middle of your ladder, what type of "bait" could you create to attract your dream customer?

Often times, companies have a front-end product but nothing more to sell on the back-end. For that, I love to look at what else they could bundle together. Could they offer a coaching program? How about a live event? What other results or value could they give their clients?

I told you earlier that Business's core issue was not a traffic or conversion problem. The only real problem is funnel problem. One of that was they had no Value Ladder. Because of that, they couldn't build out a true sales funnel. They brought people into their funnel, but then the relationship ended. People wanted to give them money, but there was no clear path for them to follow. As soon as they added those things into their business, customers naturally started to ascend the ladder, ultimately paying you and your team what they you worth.

Again, unless you have a complete Value Ladder, it's impossible to build out an effective sales funnel.

LEAD CAPTURE FUNNEL

What's up everybody! The moon is up, the rain is falling outside and I am sew excited that you guys have reached this chapter. On an average, a person reads almost 6% of book, and then never ever touch it, but you guys are sew embedded and thirsty for knowledge and success that you reached this chapter. I really appreciate that and now its the time to jump into action and create a funnel for yourself.

The funnel that we create here is the lead capture funnel, but why? Why lead gen funnel? We can ever create homepage funnels, squeeze page funnels, survey funnels etc, but why only Lead gen funnel? This is something that I learn very late. In case of CCA (coursecreationacademy.co.in) I was surviving in middle not just because less number are coming to that course, but more the impact was due to less number of revisits. We think more than once while buying something, even most of us discuss it with our family, or staff, or team before investing, so it means revisiting the site is very much important than just knowing about the site. Here we need some framework that keep reminding the potential customer to revisit the site, here to increase the sales, we must need to push the link and message to the potential customers again and again. Just like in offline sales, salesperson call potential customers again and again from the mobile phone records we made, similarly in online world we need to make record or list of email addresses, that we can easily send automated emails and remainders to the potential customers and site visitors.

This is something that I earn very late

It is said "YOUR MONEY IS IN YOUR LIST."

I have written this line in caps lock, so that you must encircle it, put it on your walls, fragment it on your arm, do anything but never forget this fact. If your business is the engine, your product is the gasoline, so list is the oxygen. You have to make it clear that a funnel cannot sell anything automatically, if their are no people to buy your product or service.

The money is in the list. This is not a new concept. But for me it was like, when I heard that, I was like, what does that mean? What does it mean? The money's in the list. Like, I don't understand that I'm in business. I sell products. I sell services, right? This is the new, you understand like the list, like the customers, the people that you have, this is your, this is your real business. Right? The fact that I was able to send her a couple of emails. Right. You guys are my list. I send emails to my list and you showed up to this event. Now I have a chance to teach you and to train you, right. The money's in the list, like that's the asset. That's the most powerful case. One of my first mentors told me that. And I was like, okay, that's kind of cool, but I don't know what that means. Like, like what is the list? Right? And the list is just a bunch of leads, right? One lead is a person, right? 10 is, is a bunch of leads, right? A hundred or a thousand. That's a list of people. Okay. And so list is the key.

I want you to understand the value of a list. Okay. What is the list actually worth? Okay. Using Simple Marketing Maths you should be making 10rs per email address in your list per month. Its a starting goal, then the numbers should increase. That's on your email list.

So they said, okay, what that means? I said, well, that means if you have a thousand people on your list, you should be able to make ten thousand rupees a month. Right. If you had 10,000 people, unless you should make about one lakh a month, if you have a one lakh people on list, 10 lac a month and so on. And so I remember hearing that and I was like, Oh my gosh, this is amazing. Now looking at these numbers, I was like, okay, well my goal, my goal? So I said, okay, this is my goal. If I can get 10,000 people on the list at 1 lakh, a month, 12 months, that's 12 lakh rupees per annul.

Remember my spam story? I told you about in a previous chapter that how I downloaded a list of people from internet and most of them filed spam report against me and I lost my Professional email address, the question arises, how do I generate leads and how do I build my own list? Okay. The question was, how do I generate leads and how do I build my own list? Okay. That was, the question running through my head. Do you have that question in the past Or you have right now, like, okay, I want, I want leads t, if we can make a dollar per month per lead, like I want a bunch of leads in my business as well. Right. And mean just thinking about that case. That was my question now became my quest. Like, okay, how do I generate leads? How do I build a list? I got to figure this out. I was working, trying to figure it out. And I was looking a bunch of stuff.

I will show you an example of "Kiss test." This experience I learn from My Buddy, my mentor, Russell Bronson.

He tells his experience like that:

I've become friends with founder of Doubleyourdating.com.

And at the time he had a business called double your dating. And he heard rumors. He don't know what the numbers were. People like say, yeah, he's making tens of millions of dollars a year and all this kind of stuff. And so he was trying to research everybody. I remember going to his website personally and I went to his website.

What I saw was something I'd never seen before. Okay. This is what the website actually looked like.

It was this little page right here. Okay. And I remember reading said, you're about to learn the secrets that most men will never know about women. And I was like, okay, as that inside, you're going to learn the kiss test. How to tell if she's ready to be kissed? I remember listening to Russell and I was like, Whoa, what is the kiss test? I go to know what that is.

Being a vision focused, a teen and totally away from stuff like that, it was kind of weird and embarrassing to show my hunger to case studies of dating, so I told my father about it, I told that I really wanna know, how this site makes money and then he replied, yes I understand, that evening, he was sitting with me when I signed up the form with my email address.

So I put mine first name and email address and I clicked submit to get instant access, to find out what the kiss test was.

Right. So I did that and I'm waiting on the next page to be blown away by like some video or some training course or something. But on the next page, all was, this is what the page looked like.

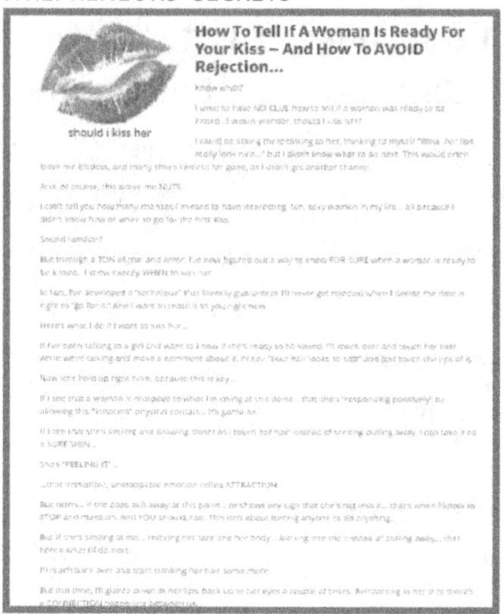

Okay. It was like an article, maybe a page and a half, two page article. And the very top, it said, this is the kiss test. Let me teach you how it works. Okay. Now again, I was focused on my vision and career and I am a nice guy. So I didn't, I hadn't been on a date outside of my parents. So I didn't, I was trying to put myself in the context, if I was a single guy who was struggling to get girls, like how valuable this information be to me. And so this is where the kiss test was. There was written; You walk a girl up to the door. Okay. And as you're sitting there, this is the awkward spot. Right? Do I kiss her? Oh, I'd have her freak out and they want to run away. Right? He said, this is the secret. He's all used to go up there and you put your hand behind her hair. Like, you're gonna put your hair behind her ear. Okay. And if she, if she pulls back, that means don't kiss her run as fast as you can. Okay. But as she turns her head into your hand, that's the key that she's ready to be kissed. And then boom, you go for the move. And that's the kiss test. I remember reading that. I was like, Oh my gosh, like that it wasn't this huge long report or PDF. It was like a paragraph. It was this little paragraph right here saying this is the kiss test.

I was like, if I was a single guy right now, I just received value. I was like, Oh my gosh. That was, that was really, really cool. What else does this guy have? And if he kept reading the page to the bottom, he's like, Hey, if you want another tip like this, go buy my Ebook called double your dating and click there. And it took you to go buy a Z book and free trail of his membership site, which had a whole bunch of different tips and secrets like that.

And I remember looking at, and I studied this over for like weeks. I'm like, this is how this guy's build this huge list. He's got this weird website that the only thing you can do is put your email address in, and next page, he gives you this really cool thing that dudes really, really want. And like, this is how he's built this huge email list of hundreds, of thousands of people. According to my personal research when I checked the site's google analytics this site is getting 1812 unique (new) visitors on an average, every single day. Its INSANE!!!

DOUBLEYOURDATING.COM TRAFFIC WORTH

We estimate the website value of **doubleyourdating.com** is currently at **$ 1,374 USD** and reaches roughly **797 unique users each day** that generate **1,882 daily pageviews** with a daily revenue (from advertisements, i.e Google AdSense) of **$ 2 USD** approximately. According to Alexa (the Web Information Company) the Global Traffic Rank is **509,833** (view Alexa traffic graphs). Read our guide to Beginner's SEO: Quick Tips to Boost Your SEO to increase traffic on your website.

It makes millions of dollars a year. And so the more I looked at it more as trying to figure out how does this work? I need to put these pieces together and what I realized, and when I kind of find out, as I started learning more about this is that this kiss test, right? This thing right here, that he had created, this is what we call a lead magnet. Key is, lead magnet is something that's going to draw. It's going to attract your dream customers to you. Okay. And a lot of you guys have heard of a lead magnet before, but this is one of the keys to building your own list is the lead magnet is something that people want. Okay. So for him, he's in the market. I need to figure out how to pick up girls. Okay. The lead magnet was the kiss test.

I'll teach you the kiss test. If you give me an email address, okay. I'm an exchange this thing for you. Okay. And that was the lead magnet. Okay. So I started thinking for my business, like, who are my dream customers? What do they look like? Like, what are those people like that I wanted to bring into my world? Who is my dream customer? I start thinking, what is the lead magnet I could create? It would get those people attracted to me, right? Where they're on the internet, surfing on their phone, swiping through. Also they saw something like, Whoa, I want that thing. I want to learn the kiss test. I want to learn the, whatever the thing is. Right? Okay. That lead magnet thing gets them to stop scrolling, click on a button, come over to you, give you their email address. And now they become a lead.

Okay. And the more leads you get, you start building this list. Okay. And the value in your business is your list. That is the key. Okay. So after seeing this, I was like, okay, this is the game. I know how to play. Now, now that I knew the rules, I knew how to play the saw I get this. I'm not spammy. People don't want to hear from me, but I'm getting people who are interested, who come to me because I have value. Okay. This is how we build the list of people actually want to hear from me.

Okay. So I did what, what, hopefully you guys gonna be doing this week, as well, as I said, okay, I'm going to go and create my first lead magnet. I'm gonna set up a lead squeeze funnel. I'm going to do exactly what he's doing. Okay. So I did that.

Okay. I modeled it as close as I could. I built up my very first lead squeeze funnel. I put it out there and I launched it. And I want to come back to these numbers because these numbers were actually interesting. Initially for me, my numbers almost sync to what I was told earlier for when my, one of my friends. Okay. I still remember the very first month that I started, I had my first lead magnet. I was driving traffic to the very first month. I got 74 people who opted in. I don't know why I remember that number. Like that's that's a lot of people would give me their email address. Now they're on an email list. I can send emails to talking about the products and services I wanted to sell.

Let me show you the exactly the first lead magnet I ever created and still it capture leads for me, emails of people that wanted to increase their conversion ratio with mine funnels.

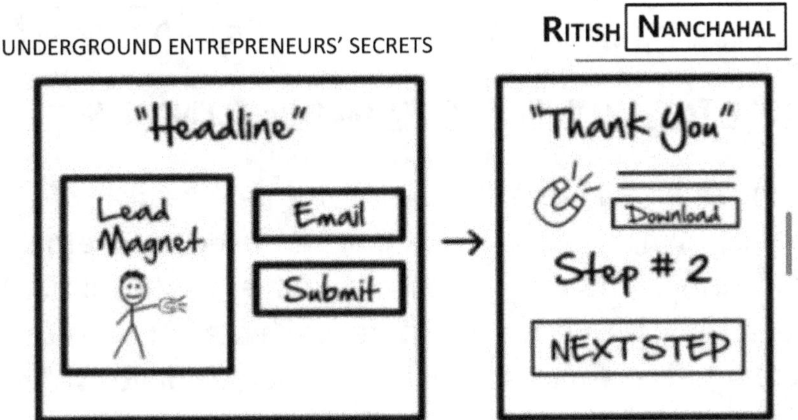

This is how my lead magnet looks like; It have a big headline delivering my message that 8x your conversion ratio, there is a way that I can teach you for free, just give me your email address and I will send you the free one page report.

As soon the viewers give there email address and submit, they are redirected to this one page report, having questions for self reflection and a video pinned on top with me training them to increase conversions and fill answers to these questions. Its damn simple and it took me less then 20 minutes to create this lead magnet.

Devoted to all non venture startups with no safety nets

HOW THIS WORKS AND ITS 6 CORE ELEMENTS

Fundamentally Lead magnet funnel consist of 2 pages simply. The first one is used for email capturing. It provides valuable information regarding the value it will deliver when the visitor submits his email address. The second page is the thank you page. After submitting the email address, the visitor, get link to download the valuable content, or we can simply add here the hyperlink of the article or stuff that you wanna deliver in exchange of the email address.

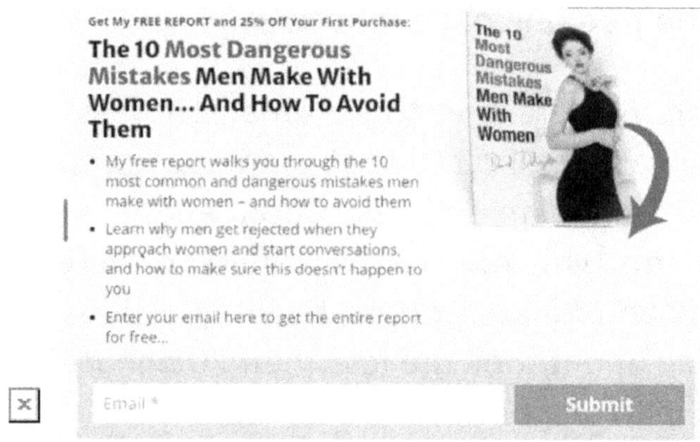

This is the another lead magnet of his site, that is still available when you visit the kiss test page. It has core elements:-

1. Irresistible Headline: Source of Attraction

2. Sales Copy: Create Awareness
3. "Get a free report" tagline: Creates Motivation for Signing up
4. A thumbnail: Removes Doubts from visitor's mind about final value he will receive after signing up
5. Email Capture Tool: Must required for your list building.
6. Time Limit (Missing here!): It pressurize them to give their email address or they will loose the value forever

The Headline creates the first and massive impact on visitor. Therefore using unnatural and thrilling headlines is strategic. Like; rather than writing "How to make money by painting" On death of the website video case study, it was written "How this

                    RITISH NANCHAHAL

nerd make 1000$ per day by painting Nude Squirrels." It was not lame, but strategic.

Creating awareness (sales-copy) for the lead capture is a really powerful tool. Not only it give the visitor to pre understand the value he will receive after giving you the email address, it also create a bridge of trust between them and your business.

Moreover, when there is something I gonna receive for free, I can never step back, and its same for everybody, right?

Moving onto the thumbnail, it makes the value visually impactful and increases probability of signing up with email address.

Time limit creates urgency, and as we know that the human attention time average per day is 7 seconds, its very profitable, if they can take decision as soon as possible.

With that said, hopefully you're moving forward on your projects and getting back to changing the world in your own little way. And with that said, I will see you in next chapter...

STEVEN LARSEN'S PURPLE OCEAN STRATEGY

I found Steven talking about this tiny but amazing concept called the purple ocean strategy. Purple ocean is actually the mix of both red ocean and blue ocean, red ocean signifies the analytics, market demands, fundamentally the science behind your business and respective approaches. blue ocean tells the story, its the art, innovation and creativity.

It can be difficult to succeed with the cutthroat competition in the business environment today. Luckily, there are many strategies you can use in order to gain an edge on your competition. Two of these are red ocean and blue ocean strategies, which were introduced by W. Chan Kim and Renee Mauborgne in 2005.

Red Ocean Strategies

A red ocean strategy involves competing in industries that are currently in existence. This often requires overcoming an intense level of competition and can often involve the commodification of the industry where companies are competing mainly on price. For this strategy, the key goals are to beat the competition and exploit existing demand.

> "The key goals of the red ocean strategy are to beat the competition and exploit existing demand."

One industry in which a red ocean strategy would be necessary is the soft drink industry. This industry has been in existence for a long time, and there are many barriers to entry. There are industry leaders in place such as Coke and Pepsi, and there are also many smaller companies also in competition for market share. There's also limited shelf space and vending spots, well-established brand recognition of popular, current brands, and many other factors that affect new competition. This causes the soft drink industry to be very competitive to enter and succeed in.

Blue Ocean Strategies

A blue ocean strategy is based on creating demand that is not currently in existence, rather than fighting over it with other companies. You must keep in mind that there is a deeper potential of the marketplace that hasn't been explored yet. Most blue oceans are created from within red oceans by expanding existing industry boundaries. The key to a successful blue ocean strategy is finding the right market opportunity and making the competition irrelevant.

> "The key goals of the blue ocean strategy are finding the right marketing opportunity and making the competition irrelevant."

An example of a successful execution of a blue ocean strategy is the iPod. When the iPod was introduced in 2001, Steve Jobs said that "with [the] iPod, Apple has invented a whole new category of digital music player that lets you put your entire music collection in your pocket and listen to it wherever you go." Apple looked beyond what was in the market at that time and introduced a product that created a new industry in and of itself. Apple looked beyond what customers were asking for and created a successful product.

The Winning Strategic Approach

While the authors of *Blue Ocean Strategy* suggest using the latter approach, no matter which you select, there are a few things to keep in mind. First of all, it is important to remember that value creation and innovation are critical success factors. Also, remain aware of the industry that you are competing against as well as new introductions to the market that may disrupt any market share that you have attained.

I become obsessed with how to get my message across clearly and in the most beneficial way for my audience.

Steven do whatever it takes to get those connections firing in my brain. I'm fixated on making *hard to chew* concepts as SIMPLE and exciting as possible...

He is a amazing guy and true funnelhacker.

'Cause *'ain't nobody loves a yawn fest.'*

Bottom study

The Red Ocean is a PROVEN Market.

The Red Ocean is safe because you already know that people want the product. However, it's *risky* because tough competition means that you'll have to compete on price.

So the chances of you making a whole lot of money are slim – *#urgh!*

The Blue Ocean is a NEW OPPORTUNITY for your market!

The Blue Ocean is where you'll find yourself if you create an offer that's prolific – Something *different* to what's already out there.

Sure, there's a lot less competition… BUT, you're still taking a RISK – because your offer isn't proven. How do you know if *anyone actually wants it… or what they're willing to pay you for it??? Fatal Flaw Alert*

Then, it hit me!

Here's the Equation:

Red Ocean = *Product Security + Intense Competition* = **RISK**

Versus

Blue Ocean = *No Competition + Less Market Security* = **RISK**

So, what do you do…

  RITISH NANCHAHAL

How do you combine the Security of the Red Ocean with the Opportunity of the Blue Ocean? Can you minimize risk, serve more people and MAKE MORE MONEY?

Is it even possible?

Relax! This is where my pacing, dancing, and obsession pays off

'Welcome to the Purple Ocean of Opportunity'

The **Purple Ocean** is a mixture of the Red & Blue Ocean...

Think about it...

You mix the best aspects of the Red and the Blue Ocean together, and you create the Purple Ocean!

> 'The Purple Ocean provides the Security of the Red Ocean with the Opportunity of the Blue'

So, you might be thinking, *'Yeah, this sounds great Ritish, but how does it work?*

Let me explain:

Recently, when I've been putting together my offers, I've been using the Purple Ocean Concept to great effect.

My students have been feeling its impact too. It's sooo incredibly powerful!

How to Create a Purple Ocean Offer?

- When you create an offer, make sure that you take elements from the Red Ocean and combine them with elements from the Blue Ocean that you want to guide your customers towards.
- The mixture of the elements from the Red and Blue Ocean creates a **Purple Ocean Offer**. This provides the SECURITY and SAFETY of

the Red Ocean while gently guiding your customer over to the prolific NEW OPPORTUNITY of the Blue Ocean – where you have more control and less competition.

- Your customers will often guide you and let you know which elements of the Red Ocean are needed to help make them feel safe and secure.

Entrepreneur's Dilemma

'If I had asked people what they wanted, they would have said faster horses.' – Henry Ford

It's fascinating to look at the significant industry shifting products, like the iPhone, because they often follow the same **Purple Ocean** method.

Jobs had a vision of what was possible. He produced an entirely revolutionary product. However, he made sure that his product fulfilled the needs of Red Ocean customers as well as the those of the *more innovative* early adopters.

> 'You can't just ask customers what they want and then try to give that to them. By the time you get it built, they'll want something new.' -Steve Jobs

Jobs recognized the same issue as Ford and, as an entrepreneur, you need to do the same.

It's your job to hold a vision of what's possible for your customers – while adding the safety and familiarity of the Red Ocean elements to your offer.

That way you help your customers to transition to your New Offer in a stress-free way.

For Example:

If your customers are convinced that the *only* way to make phone calls is with a mobile service provider, then you have to make sure that your offer *includes* the SECURITY of that service.

You can then throw *Wi-FI calls* and *Face Time* into the mix – and gradually win them over to the NEW and the prolific.

Freaked out, scared customers who are unsure of your product are the least likely to part with their cash. They'll refuse to buy into your vision – however amazing it is.

They'll keep their money in their wallets until they find a solution that fits their preconceived ideas.

Think about how many people resisted getting an iPhone *(or even a Smart Phone)* when they first came out! It was just too much for them to take on board: *'Why would I want to Face Time anyone- my phone is enough for me.'*

One of the main reasons for this success is the Purple Ocean that my product is swimming in!

So before you create an offer stack...

Ask yourself these questions:

- Are your customers looking at your offer in a *suspicious* way because it is too prolific/ new/ revolutionary?
- What is the 'current' Red Ocean norm and is your offer too far away from it?
- What elements from the Red Ocean can you add to your stack to help your customers feel safe – to help them make the transition to your Blue Ocean more easily?

Honestly, try it — I think you'll be amazed at the structure and clarity it will give your offer creation. And, most importantly, the effect that creating a Purple Ocean of Opportunity will have on your wallet! Alright! So, that's the game plan.

I know this is going to help you CRUSH IT with your offer creation. Until next time... Go Kill It!

UNIT:-3

BOOSTING THE HORMONES

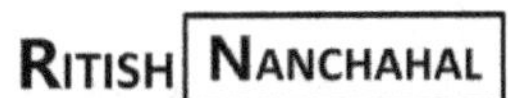

I FELT LIKE QUITTING EVERYDAY

A PIC OF ME, DEPRESSED AND CRYING DUE TO FINANCIAL CRISIS, THAT MY FATHER CAPTURED TO SHOW ME THE SWLF IMAGE AND TEACH ME TO BE HAPPY, LUCKILY THIS WAS BACHED UP TO MY DRIBE AND THIS IA HOW I AM ABLE TO TEACH YOU THE SAME

We all have diverse faces. We have those experiences, when we were feeling as a confident leader. We also remember that faces, when we were too mentally depressed and thinking of ways to commit suicide, also some faces were too aggressive that we wanna kill the frontier as well.

In my class 11, in financial crisis time, one day I was going to my class, I was depressed due to the recent conflict with my mother. At time of taking the bus, thought came; what if I will never come

Devoted to all non venture startups with no safety nets

back or this bus met with an accident, what if its end day if my life. A life is meaningless if only hardships are there, mental, financial, educational etc hardships. God showed me sign that day, as I entered the bus, people were filled like popcorn in popcorn machine. Literally that time I stood in open gate of the bus, on its second step. As the bus started increasing the speed, that one step back threatened me. Then I watched the ticket collector with a handbag full of money. Then I was like ugh!, its difficult to jump and commit suicide, rather, its much easier to make money. That time logic made more sense to me than emotions, actually emotion of fear was edge over the emotion of depression.

Its the truth that we have to do the hard things first. to get ease after...

Whatever the condition was, I made myself unstoppable. I made myself obsessed with keep moving. I was teaching tutions, restoring bikes before. I was doing everything that I can do and have interest in, As soon I jumped to entrepreneurship, I left off all other tasks and focused only on one target, creating impact and live life of abundance using my funnel strategy. I made myself fully devoted and Totally Inn. I wanna take the island, so I burnt my boats.

Its your life, your decisions, so at first put others' opinions aside.

Most people pay attention to the final product. If you fail they will call you stupid. if you win they will call you lucky. But they will never see what you have overcome and what you will overcome to reach your destiny. The struggles, the daily rejections, the headache, the hardships, the consistent failures, the disputes, the trails, rumors, criticism, debts, your empty bank account. And all those lonely nights are going to make your vision reality. Many hustlers break a lot of walls and win many wars, but they quit at a point which was the last wall between themselves and their success, ultimately, they never succeed. The only difference between one who quits and one who kept moving is not the commitment, but it's the loyalty to self decisions and commitments, the funnel hackers showed up everyday. They kept learning everyday. They kept working everyday, They kept creating funnels everyday. They learn from proven mentors, books and stuff everyday. They evolve and improve everyday. They do all this, even if they feel like quitting everyday......

And finally They became the better version of themselves, the personality, they are today......

RITISH NANCHAHAL

LEAD FUNNEL CHALLENGE

#AFUNNELAWAY

When I was working on my Course creation academy programme I sent a text to my friend Samarth and told him about the vision and concept behind it. He said that he would definitely take time for it and wanna learn how to launch an E course online. I sent him the link when it was launched but he did not registered for the class. Not only in his case I noticed the same case for many people, that once they get excited and motivated about something they invest in the product. But when that motivation overs, they became lazy and say things like I will do it tomorrow, the next day "I will do it tomorrow, I do not have time" and ultimately they never do it.

As we have seen in covid, studies are impacted, because living in home and watching recorded lectures seems to lack discipline and timing. The students who were taking live lecture, still was doing better in studies as compared to those who were watching recordings.They lack consistency and ultimately there efforts seems to be effortless and they not get the results what they were expecting, right?

That's why this time we are going to do it live. Yes, its a paid challenge and will cost you Rs 1000. Don't worry, it's not compulsory, but a life changing experience. It will not make you money, making money is work of government. It will make you a magnet that attracts money, success and abundance. If I promise you that whatever you will learn in this event will 2x your profits and growth. If you are making 10,000, you will start making 20,000, if you are making 20,000, you will start making 20,000, if you are making 40k, you will start making 80k definitely, will you give me just 1000 rs then? The Things that I gonna share will be you is insanely profitable and I guarantee you that nobody else is teaching it at this price. Even I invested 1240$, (you can calculate amount in rs) to learn what I am going to teach you there for just 1000 rs. In 5 days you will learn the whole framework behind a perfect lead magnet and at end of 4th day you will be ready to fire up and start capturing leads with your own lead magnet that you will create with your hands, isn't that amazing? And ready to start capturing leads with itself.

The timings and FAQs will be on the link given below. The schedule will be like;-

DAY 1 - Unlimited Leads

We will kick off this EXCITING challenge on DAY ONE by showing you the high level strategy that we use to be able to generate leads on demand from the internet. It will be exciting as you see how this method will work for YOUR Business, specifically Coaching or training business! This day is the only "lecture" day, everything else is workshops actually IMPLEMENTING what you learn each day!

DAY 2 - Creating Your "Lead Magnet"

Now that you've learned who your dream customers are, and how we find them, then next step is to build your first lead magnet. We will be showing you a simple process of taking your own framework, and then quickly building a "One page Report" that will act like a lead magnet to get people to come to you!

DAY 3 - Your Lead Funnel

After you've created your "One page report," the next step is to place it inside of a very simple funnel called a "Lead Squeeze Funnel." The goal of this funnel is to convert your dream customers into actual leads!

DAY 4 - Follow-Up Funnels (emails)

Now that you have leads coming into your funnel, it's essential that you quickly build a relationship with those leads. Your special guest trainer may come come and teach you the simple 6 email follow-up funnel that will build a relationship with your leads so they will be excited to buy from you in the future!

NOTE: this day you will also be given ALL EMAILS WRITTEN that you have to just copy-paste for yourself.

DAY 5 - Launch Your Funnel

Now that everything is in place, the last step is to actually launch your funnel! Today you will have another surprises or guests that will show you how to launch your funnel without paid ads! That's right, you don't need to spend money initially to get leads! You'll learn stupid simple tactics that you can use to start building your list without ads!

Every day I will be live with you guys for 2-3 hours a day and we will discuss all the strategies and doubts live. We will together level up the energy and impact. Also you will get interactive worksheets and access to my video training with that. Even I will solve those worksheets and homework with all you guys live. You will get access to my whattsap number where you can clear all your doubts and share your thoughts with me one on one by just sending a text, isn't that better than all other options in market?

https://bit.ly/3vl7L6T

Being result motivated I am ready to do whatever it takes and make you guys succeed. I can even do this challenge for free, the little fee of 1000Rs is just, so that you guys have some skin in this game, So that you take it seriously, be on time, do the homework and finally create the business you dream of, live the life of abundance that you dream of. Alright? So that's the game plan. Please make sure that we are going to do it live this time, in future its not the case that it will be available live, like this time, we can switch to recorded version again. Also there will be no playbacks and recordings available of this 5 day event. As soon it will end, everything will be taken out from the web and the site will be shut down.

https://bit.ly/3vl7L6T

SO, What are you waiting for, go and check the link and grab the seat now, since we allow less than 100 people attend this live training, so that everybody gets enough time for doubts and thought sharing, alright?

So that's the game-plan and the link is going to be down this week and the challenge is going to start, do not wait , go and grab the seats now and I will see you there......

THE STORM IS ALMOST HERE

I told you and I warned you that there's a storm coming. I want to talk about what's happening and how to prepare.

Hope you guys are doing awesome. All right. So I know this is like the last 12 months of our life, there's just so much chaos, so much craziness happening. We've had social networks shutting people down. We've had investment things and different living procedures. There's just so much chaos coming around and I don't even know how to address all the things. I'm going to try to address all the things.

All I'm going to tell you guys is when I was writing this book , in the intro, if you remember the intro book says, "There's a storm coming..." We got to start preparing ourselves for that today. And I just know that it's getting crazier and scary.

Anyway, I'm very excited because last night when I was getting ready for bed, I opened up Whats App real quick and I'm scrolling around, and one of my buddies, Ansh replied to my status and I wanted to actually read that to you because it is exactly what's been on my mind for the last week or two.

I was at the time trying to figure out how to get free employees. I emailed my list, "Hey, who wants to come work for me for free for a month and I will teach you funnels as a deal?" And he replied. He asked, how it would be worthy? I said, "I ain't smart enough to know what's going on, but I ain't dumb enough to not see something's going on. You know what I mean?"

He said 'No', I told him "I ain't panicking, but I am preparing, turning as many rupees to mental assets. For me, that means knowledge currency and stuff, that will not make me dependable on others for my life. Like the multiple ways to create traffic, like SEO, email subscribers, and social following. Layers of redundancy. If they cut off the ads, I have SEO. If they cut off social, I still have email. I am learning marketing, I read books, I write them too and this is how I can create multiple chains of making money.I plan for the best, but I have confidence of facing the worst as well.

Some people mix it up with my other thinking that burn your boats, if you wanna take the island theory. But we cannot fit one formula everywhere. It makes you not to leave your niche and focus from a business and shift it to somewhere else. Like if today you felt somebody is making money with

  Ritish Nanchahal

rearing goats, you started doing , then you found advertising agency is making millions, you start an advertising company, that should not be there. It can be seen by the vector sum of your energy and focus. The biggest reason why most people fail, because they are taking random actions, they got attracted by shiny things, they give inputs in random directions, that's why they get random result and a totally messed up random life.

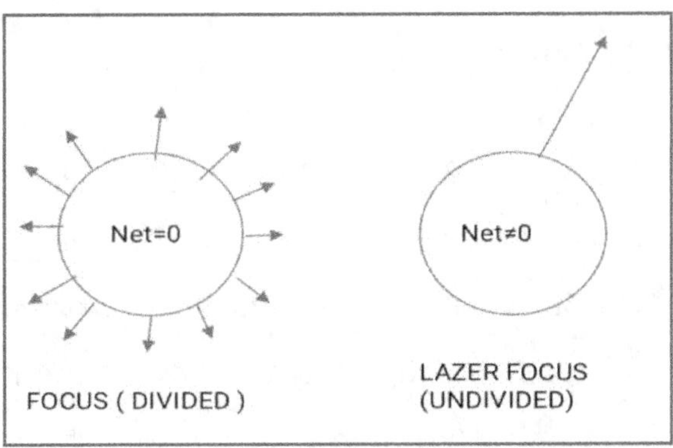

Weather if I only focus on advertising agency so each and every time when I think of growth, I will get similar ideas, relative beliefs, like running campaigns, creating coupons, changing colour scheme of banners, modifying copy etc. So inputs are directive, similarly I will get directive results.

I WANT SOME OF MY DREAM CLIENTS TO MAKE FUNNELS TOGETHER

"I'm Looking For A Few More Of My Dream Clients – Who I Can Personally Work With To Build Out Their New "Break Even" Funnel...

Why I am Doing This?

I never get care and love from my grandparents. My father was the only child of them but their nature was like to feed children of their friends' families and never ever asked about the health of us even when my father was surviving with epilepsy and brain haemorrhage, even living in the same home they never asked about health and cared. Me and my family have different nature. Even after knowing that grandparents have lend all the property to someone else. They are not thinking about our future, we still come back after some years to live with them. To take care of them and earn for them, But they like to abuse us in front of others, take old assets from other people but never ready to get beloved by us and use our money and stuff. I cannot share all the story here, my fingers are shaking. I am in intense pain, but in one line I can write Where commonly children became against parents in adulthood due to greed of properties, due to fear of living together and taking responsibility of parents, it was opposite in our case, we want to live with them, take their responsibility, we even do not want any money or property from them, but they were heartless and one day I listened my grandmother talking to her friend on phone, that she is feeling insecure living with us and will feel better, when four of us will die...

That was a kind of devastating day for me.

I was emotionally broke, mentally broke and financially broken. That loneliness, something missing in life pushed me to create opportunities for others like me, Who have potential inside, who can change the world and can impact others with their talks, products and services. That's why I am doing what I am doing today. Its my mission to impact ! million lives and I want you, to book a session with me and create your business or boost up your business if you already have with funnels. Remember your life, your abundance, your dreams, your family will be fed by the business you have created, I will wait for your call. You are just A FUNNEL APART......................

NEXT STEP

1. Go to THE SPECIAL LINK and book a strategy discussion right now to design a clear cut strategy for your business's growth or new startup. Become my dream client and get a chance to co-host upcoming events with me.
 LINK

2.   Follow me on Instagram with my handle @hackritish to remain updated with the funnel stuff, motivation, and strategies.

3. If you literally want to change your business and serious about the self investment and chasing your dreams (you should , if you read this book), you must apply for the 5 day LEAD FUNNEL CHALLENGE to get your current situation into momentum with your success side. LINK

4. Get on fire, learn from the 5 day lead challenge and learn to create and run your own lead magnet campaign.

Devoted to all non venture startups with no safety nets

+++++**<u>END</u>**+++++

Devoted to all non venture startups with no safety nets

Devoted to all non venture startups with no safety nets

Devoted to all non venture startups with no safety nets